THE KINGFISHER
ILLUSTRATED POCKET
THESAURUS

KINGFISHER

a Houghton Mifflin Company imprint
222 Berkeley Street
Boston, Massachusetts 02116
www.houghtonmifflinbooks.com

First published in 2008
2 4 6 8 10 9 7 5 3 1
1TR/0407/PROSP/PICA(PICA)/120WF

Author: Susan Harvey
Editor: Marcus Hardy
Coordinating editor: Stephanie Pliakas
Designer: Ray Bryant
Illustrations by: David Ashby (Garden Studio), Julian Baker,
Julie Banyard, Ian Howatson, Mark Iley, Josephine Martin
(Garden Studio), Clive Spong (Linden Studio)
DTP coordinator: Catherine Hibbert
DTP operator: Claire Cessford
Production controller: Teresa Wood
Proofreader: Susan Buckheit

LIBRARY OF CONGRESS CATALOGING-IN-PUBLICATION DATA
has been applied for.

ISBN 978-0-7534-6117-4

Printed in China

THE KINGFISHER
ILLUSTRATED POCKET
THESAURUS

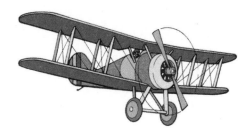

KINGFISHER
BOSTON

Introduction

Why do we use a thesaurus?

A thesaurus is a book of words, but it isn't the same thing as a dictionary. Dictionaries tell you what words mean; a thesaurus doesn't give meanings or definitions of words, but instead groups together words that have similar meanings. A word that means the same thing as another word is called a synonym, so a thesaurus is a dictionary of synonyms. The word *thesaurus* comes from a Greek word meaning "treasury" or "a place where a treasure is stored."

Why do we need to know lots of words that mean the same thing? What's wrong with using the same words all the time? We could certainly survive using the same few words—we would usually be able to ask for what we want and have conversations with our friends and family. But we would soon find that our conversations had become boring, and we might not be able to explain *exactly* what we want or say *precisely* what we mean. Nor would we want to read stories where the same words are used over and over again; that would become tedious.

English is a very rich language; it has hundreds of thousands of different words, and most of these words are synonyms of other words. By using a variety of words instead of sticking to the same ones all the time, we can make our speech and writing more interesting. Think of the word *nice*; it's a very common English word because it can apply to so many things—there's *nice weather*, *a nice person*, *a nice house*, and you can have *a nice time*. It's such a general word that it doesn't give you much information at all, and you would soon become bored if you were reading a story where everything was *nice*. It's much more interesting to read or hear about *warm, sunny weather*, *a friendly person*, *a magnificent house*, and *an enjoyable time*. All of these adjectives are synonyms of *nice*, yet they give so much more information and help you picture the scene in your imagination.

How to use this thesaurus

This thesaurus will help you make your speaking and especially your written work much more interesting. Imagine that you are writing a ghost story. You might find that you keep using the words *scared* and *afraid* and your story is beginning to sound repetitious. Look up the words *scared* and *afraid* in this thesaurus; you'll find all of the main words, or headwords, written in alphabetical order, just like in a dictionary. The meanings of the words aren't given, but the words are used in sentences, so you can be sure that you've got the right sense of the word. When you find *scared*, you'll see that you are given the four synonyms *afraid*, *frightened*, *petrified*, and *terrified*. You had already thought up *afraid* yourself, but now you've got three new words that you can use in your story. When you find *afraid*, you'll see that there are two sentences written out, each giving a slightly different meaning of the word *afraid*. Read the sentences to see which one is closer in meaning to what you want to say. Let's assume it's the first context, since you're writing a ghost story. You're given the synonyms *alarmed*, *fearful*, *frightened*, *scared*, and *terrified*, two of which, *alarmed* and *fearful*, are new, so now you have a total of five new words to include in your story. The words in parentheses after *alarmed* (*at/by*) mean that, although you say *frightened of*, *afraid of*, *terrified of*, and so on, you have to say *alarmed at* or *alarmed by*.

As well as the example sentences, which will help you choose the correct sense of the headword, parts of speech are also given. If you are looking for a synonym for *answer* in the sentence *I couldn't answer the question*, you'll see that *answer* appears twice as a headword in this thesaurus, once as a noun and once as a verb. In your sentence, *answer* is a verb, so you can choose one of the two synonyms given under the entry. Your new sentence could be *I replied to the question* or *I responded to the question*.

The parts of speech listed in the thesaurus are as follows: *adj.* = adjective; *adv.* = adverb; *conj.* = conjunction; *n.* = noun; *prep.* = preposition; *v.* = verb. When you see *pl.* next to *n.*, it means that the noun is plural.

Sometimes a whole phrase is offered as a synonym of a word. If you're searching for a synonym for *nosy*, you'll see that you can replace the word *nosy* in the phrase *He's so nosy* with *curious*, *inquisitive*, *intrusive*, *meddlesome*, or *prying* in any piece of writing and with *snoopy* in an informal context.

A few words of warning
You'll see that some synonyms are described as formal, informal, literary, or old-fashioned. Informal words may not be suitable for a serious piece of written work, but may be fine if you are preparing an oral presentation on a subject. Literary or old-fashioned words may be okay for a story or a report, but may be inappropriate in an

informal letter to a friend. If you are unsure about how exactly a word is used—maybe you've never seen the word before—then look up the word in your *Kingfisher Illustrated Pocket Dictionary* to find the exact meaning and check that it is suitable.

Although one word may have several synonyms, this doesn't mean that all synonyms mean exactly the same thing and give the reader exactly the same picture or sense. The English language is not always like a jigsaw puzzle, where one word can be taken out of a sentence and a synonym put in its place without affecting the overall picture. Often there are feelings or emotions attached to words that are very important. The words *damp* and *moist* have identical definitions in *The Kingfisher Illustrated Pocket Dictionary*—"slightly wet." Yet we talk about someone having *nice, moist skin*, while a house can be *horrible and damp*; *moist* is a positive word, whereas *damp* in this phrase conjures up a negative picture. *The Kingfisher Illustrated Pocket Thesaurus* highlights many of these differences in meaning, so check that you've got the right sense before you use a synonym in your writing. Keep your *Kingfisher Illustrated Pocket Dictionary* alongside your thesaurus at all times so that you can check the meanings of any unfamiliar synonyms that you come across.

Other information in this thesaurus

A pronunciation guide is given next to words that can be pronounced differently depending on their meaning. This will help you find the correct headword if you are unsure of the part of speech of the word that you are looking up.

As well as synonyms being given for each headword, for some words an antonym (or opposite) is listed too. Antonyms are written in bold type and are preceded by an asterisk (*). All of the antonyms are headwords in the thesaurus, so you can look them up and increase your vocabulary even further, which will make your written work even more interesting.

The thesaurus also contains many useful illustrations—for example, different types of ships and musical instruments. Strictly speaking, these are not synonyms; a flute is not the same as a clarinet, and a ferry is not a synonym for a liner. Nevertheless, these lists will help in schoolwork and in vocabulary building with specific topics.

Aa

ability *n.* *She has the ability to do very well in her career.* aptitude, capacity, intelligence, potential, skill, talent

able *adj.* *He is a very able boy.* capable, clever, competent, gifted, intelligent, proficient, skillful, talented
I'm not able to come to the game. allowed to, free to, in a position to **unable

abolish *v.* *The students voted to abolish the school uniform.* cancel, do away with, eliminate, get rid of, put an end to, scrap (*informal*) **keep

about¹ *prep.* *I borrowed a book about dinosaurs.* concerning, dealing with, regarding, relating to, to do with, touching on

about² *adv.* *We have about $20 between us.* almost, approximately, around, nearly

above¹ *prep.* *Above our heads is a shelf.* on top of, over
She's in the class above me. ahead of, beyond, higher than **below

above² *adv.* *The stars up above shone brightly.* high up, on high, overhead, aloft (*literary*) **below

abrupt *adj.* *The horse came to an abrupt stop.* hasty, hurried, sudden, unexpected
The boss wrote a very abrupt e-mail. blunt, brusque, curt, gruff, offhand, terse **friendly

absent *adj.* *Salma has been absent all week.* away, elsewhere, missing, not present **present

absent-minded *adj.* *The absent-minded professor wore one black shoe and one brown shoe.* distracted, forgetful, inattentive, preoccupied **attentive

absolute *adj.* *That's absolute garbage!* complete, total, utter

absolutely *adv.* *We had an absolutely wonderful time.* completely, perfectly, quite, totally, utterly

abuse¹ *n.* (*uh-byoos*) *We must stop the abuse of animals.* harm, mistreatment **care
There is no place for abuse on the football field. curses, insults, swear words, mudslinging (*informal*)
A serious abuse of power invites dire consequences. exploitation, misuse

abuse² *v.* (*uh-byooz*) *We should never abuse animals.* harm, hurt, injure, mistreat **protect
The crowd started abusing the players. curse, insult, swear at **flatter
The supervisor abused his power. exploit, misuse, take advantage of

accent *n. The accent is on the first syllable.* beat, emphasis, rhythm, stress
Patrick speaks with a strong Irish accent. brogue, drawl, pronunciation, twang

accept *v. Sue accepted the job.* receive, take, take on *turn down*
They had to accept the referee's decision. acknowledge, comply with, consent to, recognize *reject*

accident *n. There has been a terrible accident on the bridge.* calamity, collision, crash, disaster, mishap
I came across the website by accident. chance, coincidence, luck

account *n. The witness gave a full account of the accident.* description, narrative, record, report, statement, story

accurate *adj. The book contains some very accurate descriptions of how people lived in Colonial times.* correct, exact, factual, faithful, precise

accuse *v. They accused her of theft.* blame (for), charge (with), denounce (for) *defend*

ache[1] *n. I've got a dull ache in my lower back.* pain, twinge

ache[2] *v. My leg aches.* be painful, be sore, hurt, sting

achieve *v. I've achieved all of my goals.* accomplish, attain, fulfill, reach

achievement *n. What an incredible achievement—we're all extremely proud of you.* accomplishment, attainment, deed, exploit, feat

act[1] *n. One act of kindness can go far.* action, deed, feat, presentation
The stage is already set for the next act. performance, presentation, turn

act[2] *v. The medicine acted quickly.* function, operate, take effect, work
I've never acted on the stage before. appear, perform

action *n. The police officer was praised for her brave actions.* act, deed, exploit, feat, undertaking
The movie is full of action. activity, drama, excitement, movement

actual *adj. The scientist checked the actual noise levels.* certain, concrete, correct, genuine, real, true

adapt *v. It did not take Matthew very long to adapt to his new school.* accommodate oneself, adjust, conform, fit in, get used to

add *v. Add all of the numbers in the first column.* count, count up, total
Arun added more pages to his project. affix, append, attach,

connect *detach

adjust v. It is possible to adjust the height of the chair. alter, amend, correct, modify, rectify, regulate
Our puppy quickly adjusted to her new home. accommodate oneself, adapt, conform, fit in, get used to

admire v. I admire you for saying what you believe. applaud, appreciate, approve of, hold in high esteem, look up to, respect *disapprove

admit v. Nonmembers will not be admitted. allow entry, allow in, grant access, let in *exclude
He admitted that he had broken the window. acknowledge, confess, own up *deny

adore v. She adores her children. admire, idolize, love, revere, worship *hate

adult adj. Just over half of the adult population of France is married. full-grown, fully grown, grown-up, mature

advance v. Good weather conditions meant that the troops were able to advance quickly across the desert. go on, move forward, proceed, progress
We must work very hard to advance freedom and human rights. develop, further, increase, promote *hinder
The bank advanced us the money needed to buy our new

house. lend, loan *borrow

advanced adj. She is always up on the advanced technology. latest, modern, up-to-date *old-fashioned

advantage n. Laptops have many advantages. asset, benefit, boon, good point, strength *disadvantage

adventure n. It was a fantastic adventure being in the caves. escapade, experience, undertaking, venture

advice n. My mother has always been able to give me good advice. counsel, guidance, recommendations, suggestions

advise v. His wife advised him to go to the doctor. counsel, recommend, suggest, urge

affair n. The government handled the affair badly. business, incident, matter, situation

affect v. The speech he gave did not affect my opinion on the matter at all. change, have an effect on, have an impact on, influence, sway

affection n. She is regarded with a great degree of affection by all of her students. admiration, feeling, fondness, liking, love, tenderness

affectionate adj. The children are always very affectionate. fond, loving, tender, warm-hearted

afraid adj. They're afraid of the dark. alarmed (at/by), fearful,

frightened, scared, terrified
*brave
*He is afraid to raise his hand
in front of the rest of the class.*
hesitant, reluctant, shy, timid,
unwilling *confident

after *prep. Can you please come
see me after class?* following,
later than, succeeding *before
You're after me in the line.
behind, following *before

again *adv. Let's do it again.*
afresh, anew, once more
*You'll want to watch this movie
again and again.* frequently,
often, repeatedly

against *prep. The demonstrators
at the protest were against
nuclear power.* anti, opposed
to, resistant to, versus

age[1] *n. The Victorian age is
known for its ornamental décor.*
era, period, time

age[2] *v. We've all begun to age a
lot in the past ten years.* grow
old, mature

agent *n. My agent negotiated the
contract.* go-between,
middleman, representative

aggressive *adj. Her behavior was
very aggressive.* hostile,
offensive, pushy, violent,
warlike *friendly

agony *n. He was crying in agony.*
anguish, distress, pain,
suffering, torment

agree *v. My parents and I never
agree about anything.* concur,

see eye to eye *disagree
*The witnesses' accounts did not
agree.* accord, fit, harmonize,
match
*Both sides involved in the
dispute have agreed to have
another meeting.* assent, be
willing, consent

agreement *n. An agreement about
the matter was finally reached.*
assent, concord, harmony,
understanding

ahead[1] *adv. He went on ahead.*
forward, in advance, in the
lead, onward *behind

ahead[2] *prep. We are ahead of you
in line.* in advance of, in front
of *behind

aim[1] *n. The aim of today's lesson
is to improve your computer
skills.* goal, intention, object,
objective, purpose, target

aim[2] *v. She will aim her speech
toward the young voters.* direct,
project, target

airplane *n. The airplane landed
on the runway.* aircraft, flying
machine

alarm *v. I didn't want to alarm
you by calling late at night.*
disturb, frighten, scare, startle,
worry

alert *adj. I went to bed very late
last night, so I'm not very alert
this morning.* attentive, awake,
vigilant, wakeful, watchful
*sleepy

alike *adj. The two sisters

look alike. identical, similar
*different

all¹ *adj. All of the students at the school have to wear a uniform.* each, every
It rained all week. complete, entire, whole

all² *adv. He turned in his essay once the spelling errors were all fixed.* completely, totally, wholly

allow *v. Beth's parents didn't allow her to go to the party.* give/grant permission, let, permit ***forbid**

all right *adj. I thought that the movie was all right.* acceptable, adequate, fairly good, satisfactory, okay (*informal*)
It was awful at the time, but I'm all right now. safe, unharmed, unhurt, okay (*informal*) ***hurt**

almost *adv. It's almost two o'clock.* approximately, just about, nearly, not quite, practically

alone *adj. Were you all alone in the house?* by yourself, on your own ***together**
I sometimes feel very alone. isolated, lonely, lonesome, solitary, forlorn (*literary*)

Aircraft

Hot-air balloon

Microlight

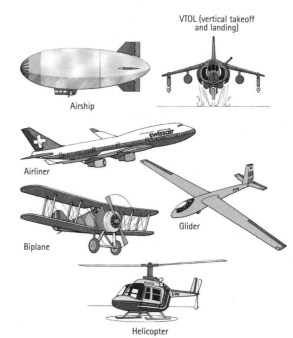

Airship

VTOL (vertical takeoff and landing)

Airliner

Glider

Biplane

Seaplane

Helicopter

already *adv. So many things had already happened.* by now, by this time, earlier, previously

also *adv. She also likes dancing.* as well, besides, furthermore, in addition, too

alter *v. I'm not planning to alter any of my vacation plans.* amend, change, modify, redesign, vary ***preserve**

altogether *adv. I'm not altogether sure that you've understood me.* completely, outright, totally, wholly

always *adv. We always visit my grandparents on Sundays.* constantly, invariably, unfailingly, without fail ***never**

I will always love you. endlessly, eternally, forever, for good, permanently, evermore (*literary*) ***never**

amateur¹ *adj. He plays on an amateur baseball team.* beginner, inexperienced, unprofessional, untrained ***professional**

amateur² *n. Don't listen to him— he's just an amateur.* learner, novice, recruit, rookie (*informal*)

amazing *adj. It was an amazing party.* fantastic, incredible, sensational, spectacular, wonderful ***ordinary**

ambition *n. Lily's ambition is to be a ballet dancer.* aim, aspiration,

Alphabets

Arabic

Japanese

Cyrillic (Russian)

АБВГДЕ

Latin

ABCDEF

Egyptian hieroglyphs

Runes

Greek

ΑΒΓΔΕΖ

Sanskrit

Hebrew

Thai

desire, dream, goal, wish

amount *n. I've got the same amount of money as you.* figure, number, quantity, sum, volume

amuse *v. I thought that this book might amuse you.* beguile, charm, delight, entertain, please

ancient *adj. We visited some ancient ruins.* historic, old *modern

anger *n. The people were demonstrating to show their anger with the plans of the government.* annoyance, fury, indignation, rage, resentment, ire (*formal or literary*), wrath (*formal or literary*) *pleasure

angry *adj. His bad behavior made me so angry.* annoyed, exasperated, furious, incensed, indignant, infuriated, irate, livid, mad, upset, steamed up (*informal*), wrathful (*formal or literary*) *calm

animal *n. The lion is an animal.* beast, creature

announce *v. The teacher announced the date of the test.* broadcast, declare, proclaim, reveal

annoy *v. It doesn't take much to annoy him.* anger, bother, displease, infuriate, irritate, upset, vex *please

annoyed *adj. My dad was annoyed at being interrupted.* angry, displeased, indignant, irritated,

upset, vexed, peeved (*informal*), ticked off (*informal*) *pleased

answer[1] *n. That was a good answer.* rejoinder, reply, response, retort, solution *question

answer[2] *v. Would you answer the question, please?* reply to, respond to *ask

anxious *adj. I got anxious when they didn't arrive.* afraid, apprehensive, concerned, fearful, nervous, worried

apologize *v. He apologized for being late.* express regret, say sorry

appeal *v. They appealed to me for help.* ask, beg, entreat, plead with, request
Horror movies don't really appeal to me. attract, interest, tempt

appear *v. A figure appeared far away.* become visible, come into sight/view, emerge *disappear
She may appear happy, but I know for a fact that she's very sick. come across as, give the impression of being, look, seem

appearance *n. Receptionists must have a neat appearance.* image, impression, look

apply *v. How can I apply my new skills to the job?* employ, make use of, use, utilize

apply oneself *v. It would be better if you applied yourself more to your work.* dedicate oneself,

Apes

Gibbon

Gorilla

Chimpanzee

Orangutan

devote oneself, show
commitment, show dedication,
work hard

appreciate *v. I really appreciate
everything you've done for me.*
admire, be grateful for, respect,
think highly of, value

appropriate *adj. To do a job well,
you should use the appropriate
tools.* apt, correct, fitting,
proper, relevant, suitable
*He used appropriate language
around the principal.* clean,
inoffensive, proper
*inappropriate

approve *v. My parents don't
approve of smoking.* admire,
agree with, appreciate, be in

favor of, favor ***disapprove**

approximate *adj. Give me an
approximate figure.* close,
estimated, rough, ballpark
(*informal*)

approximately *adv. There were
approximately 100 people.*
about, around, roughly

area *n. Our school is in a
respectable area.* district,
locality, neighborhood, place,
region, zone

argue *v. Some people argue
that the press is to blame.*
assert, claim, contend,
maintain, reason
*William and Ben argue about
everything.* bicker, disagree,
fight, quarrel, quibble, squabble

argument *n. I heard them having
an argument.* disagreement,
dispute, fight, quarrel, squabble

around¹ *prep. There are trees all
around the house.* encircling, on
every side of, surrounding

around² *adv. There was no one
around.* close by, in the vicinity,
near, nearby
*He had around 3,000 comic
books.* about, almost,
approximately, nearly

arrange *v. She arranged the
flowers in the vase.* order,
organize, put in order,
sort
*Should we arrange the meeting
for Wednesday?* fix, organize,
plan, schedule ***cancel**

arrest v. *The police arrested the thief.* capture, detain, seize, take into custody, take prisoner ***release**

arrive v. *We arrived home late.* appear, get to, put in an appearance, reach, show up (*informal*) ***depart**

arrogant adj. *What an extremely arrogant person!* conceited, disdainful, haughty, proud, self-important, supercilious, cocky (*informal*) ***modest**

article n. *Articles of value were found in the trash.* item, object, product, thing
Have you read this article? essay, feature, piece, report

artificial adj. *It's not real; it's artificial.* counterfeit, fake, false, imitation, man-made, mock, synthetic ***real**

ashamed adj. *Sally felt ashamed at what she had done.* abashed, embarrassed, guilty, red-faced, shamefaced ***proud**

ask v. *If you want anything, please ask.* appeal, demand, inquire, query, request ***answer**

assault[1] n. *His harsh words were like a verbal assault.* attack, confrontation

assault[2] v. *The thugs assaulted the taxi driver.* attack, beat up, pounce on

assortment n. *There's an assortment of cookies in the jar.* array, mixture, range, selection, variety

assume v. *I assume you're going to the party.* believe, imagine, presume, suppose
The Bolsheviks assumed power in 1917. accept, confiscate, seize, take, take over, take possession of

attach v. *Attach the cable to your computer.* affix, connect, fasten, join, link, tie ***unfasten**

attack v. *A group of bullies attacked Alex.* ambush, assault, beat up, pounce on, set upon ***defend**
Rebel groups attacked security headquarters. ambush, begin an assault, charge, descend upon, invade, raid, storm ***defend**

attempt v. *Don't attempt to lift this on your own.* endeavor, strive, tackle, try

attentive adj. *The students were attentive and asked the teacher lots of questions.* alert, heedful, intent, observant ***absent-minded**

attitude n. *The study looks closely at the attitudes of young people.* opinion, point of view, viewpoint

attract v. *Some plants attract wildlife into the garden.* draw, exert a pull on, influence, pull, tempt

attractive adj. *She's so attractive!* appealing, beautiful, good-looking, gorgeous, handsome, pretty, stunning ***ugly**

available adj. *The latest catalog is*

now available. accessible, attainable, convenient, handy, obtainable, ready, within reach

average *adj. The class discussed the average age of students' parents.* normal, standard, typical, usual **unusual*
I thought that the movie was only average. all right, mediocre, ordinary, nothing to write home about (*informal*), so-so (*informal*) **excellent*

avoid *v. I do my best to avoid him.* dodge, elude, evade, keep away from, shun, stay clear of
Pregnant women are advised to avoid alcohol. abstain from, forgo, give up, refrain from

aware *adj. I'm not aware of any problems.* conscious, informed, mindful **unaware*

away¹ *adj. Tara is away today.* absent, elsewhere, not present **present*

away² *adv. She looked away.* aside, in a different direction

awful *adj. An awful thing happened to me—my car was stolen.* atrocious, horrendous, horrible, horrid, terrible, unpleasant **wonderful*

awkward *adj. I find this vacuum cleaner really awkward to use.* clumsy, difficult, inconvenient, tricky, uncomfortable, ungainly, unwieldy **easy*
I hope I'm not calling at an awkward time. difficult,

inappropriate, inconvenient **convenient*

Bb

back¹ *n. The garden to the mansion is situated at the back of the main house.* rear, rear side **front*

back² *v. Politicians backed the smoking ban.* endorse, favor, support, uphold

bad *adj. We had really bad weather on our vacation.* appalling, atrocious, awful, terrible, rotten (*informal*) **fine*
His behavior during the lesson was bad. disobedient, disruptive, mischievous, naughty, unruly, wicked **good*
It was a very bad accident. grave, serious, severe, terrible **minor*
This barrel is full of bad apples. decayed, rotten, spoiled **fresh*

bag *n. I carry my books to school in a bag.* backpack, briefcase, knapsack

ball *n. They were playing with a beach ball.* globe, orb, sphere
Cinderella had to leave the ball at the stroke of midnight. dance, function, masquerade, party, social

ballot *n. Workers at the factory*

held a ballot. election, franchise, poll, vote

ban *v. Some people would like to ban all advertising.* bar, disallow, forbid, prohibit, stop, veto *****allow**

band[1] *n. The sailor's cap was blue with a red band.* line, strip, stripe
Robin Hood had a band of men. company, ensemble, gang, group, party, troop
I played in the school band. ensemble, orchestra

band[2] *v. Let's band together for solidarity.* assemble, collect, gather, unite

bang *v. The teacher banged on the table.* beat, crash, hammer, pound, slam, thump

bank *n. The bank of the river was muddy.* coast, edge, embankment, shore, side

bar *v. They were barring his way.* block, blockade, obstruct, prevent *****admit**

bare *adj. The walls were completely bare.* empty, plain, unadorned
He walked around the wet field in bare feet. naked, nude, unclothed, uncovered

barely *adv. There's barely enough room in the house for everyone.* hardly, just, scarcely

barrier *n. The police put a barrier across the road.* barricade, block, obstacle, obstruction

base[1] *n. The base of the statue was made of marble.* bottom, foot, foundation, pedestal, stand *****top**

base[2] *v. The company is based in Boston.* establish, locate, position, situate

beach *n. The children were playing on the beach.* sand, seaside, shore

bear *v. I can't bear it when I have to wait in lines.* accept, endure, put up with, stand, tolerate
Will this chair bear my weight? bolster, carry, hold, support

beat *v. The cruel old man regularly beat the dog with a stick.* batter, hit, pound, pummel, strike, thrash, thump
My heart was beating really fast. flutter, pound, pulsate, throb
Our team beat the other side easily. conquer, defeat, win against, lick (*informal*)

beautiful *adj. What an absolutely beautiful baby!* attractive, gorgeous, handsome, lovely, pretty *****ugly**

beauty *n. Helen of Troy's beauty caused the Trojan War.* attractiveness, good looks, grace, loveliness

because *conj. I'm going home because I'm feeling sick.* as, due to the fact that, for the reason that, owing to the fact that, seeing that, since

before *prep. You arrived here before me.* earlier than, in advance of, prior to ***after** *I'm before you in the line.* ahead of, in front of, preceding ***after**

beg *v. The children begged their grandmother to read them a story.* ask, beseech, entreat, plead with, press, request

begin *v. If you're ready, we'll begin the lesson.* embark on, launch into, make a start on, start, commence *(formal)* ***end**

beginner *n. This class is mostly made up of beginners.* apprentice, novice, recruit, trainee, rookie *(informal)* ***expert**

beginning *n. The beginning of the story is the best part.* opening, outset, start, starting point, commencement *(formal)* ***end**

behavior *n. Everyone in the school had heard about his bad behavior.* bearing, conduct, demeanor, manners

behind¹ *adv. I followed on behind.* after, afterward, at the back, following, in the rear, later ***ahead**

behind² *prep. The cat is behind the door.* at the back of, beyond *Their financial troubles are behind them.* beyond, in a time gone by, past

belief *n. Stick to your beliefs!* conviction, creed, faith, opinion, view

believe *v. The teacher believed his story.* accept, be convinced by, have confidence in, have faith in *I believe you might have known my mother.* imagine, suppose, suspect, think

below *prep. Please sign your name below mine.* beneath, lower than, under, underneath ***above**

bend *v. The road bends a little farther on.* curve, incline, swerve, turn, veer

benefit *n. The new gym is for the benefit of the whole school.* advantage, good, interest, profit, welfare ***disadvantage**

bent *adj. This wire is bent.* crooked, curved, distorted, out of shape, twisted ***straight**

besides¹ *prep. There will be other people there besides our class.* apart from, excluding, in addition to, other than

besides² *adv. It's too late to go now; besides, it's starting to rain.* anyhow, anyway, furthermore, moreover

Bells

Belfry
Bell tower
Bicycle bell
Church bell
Doorbell
Gong
Hand bell

best *adj.* *That's the best meal I've ever eaten.* finest, greatest, supreme, top, unrivaled ***worst**

better *adj.* *This bag is better quality than the cheaper one.* finer, preferable, superior ***worse**

beware *v.* *Beware of the dog.* be careful of, guard against, heed, mind, watch out for

big *adj.* *Canada is a very big country.* colossal, enormous, gigantic, huge, immense, large, vast ***small**
Toby had some big decisions to make about his career. crucial, important, major, significant, vital ***minor**

bit *n.* *Could I have a bit of cheese, please?* chunk, crumb, fragment, morsel, piece, portion

bite *v.* *The monkey tried to bite through the rope.* chew, chomp, gnaw, munch, nibble

bitter *adj.* *This juice has a bitter taste.* acidic, harsh, sour, tart ***sweet**
Paul felt bitter about the treatment that he'd received from his family. angry, embittered, resentful, sour, upset

blame *v.* *I don't blame you for what happened.* accuse, charge, condemn, criticize, hold responsible

bleak *adj.* *The house is situated in a very bleak spot.* bare, desolate, dismal, exposed ***hopeful**

block¹ *n.* *A block of wood sat on his workbench.* bar, chunk, lump, slab

block² *v.* *There was a very large crowd blocking her way when she arrived at the theater.* bar, hinder, impede, obstruct, restrict ***admit**

blue *adj.* *She was wearing blue shoes.* aquamarine, azure, cobalt, indigo, navy, turquoise
He was feeling blue today. depressed, sad, sorrowful

blush *v.* *Harry blushed whenever anyone spoke to him.* color, flush, redden, turn red

boast *v.* *He's always boasting about how rich he is.* bluster, brag, crow, gloat, show off, swagger

body *n.* *They found a body in the tunnel.* carcass, corpse, remains
The human body is an amazing machine. figure, form, physique, shape

The Body

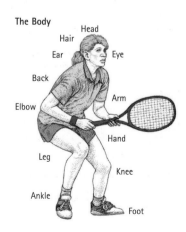

Head
Hair
Ear
Eye
Back
Arm
Elbow
Hand
Leg
Knee
Ankle
Foot

bog *n. We had to wade through the bog.* marsh, morass, quagmire, swamp

boil *v. Boil the vegetables for ten minutes.* cook, poach, simmer, steam

After the underwater explosion, the water began to boil. bubble, foam, froth, seethe

bold *adj. The bold prince found Sleeping Beauty.* adventurous, brave, courageous, daring, fearless *****cowardly**

bolt *v. We always bolt the door before we go to bed.* bar, fasten, lock, secure

The horse bolted at the sound of the helicopter. flee, run away, start, take flight

bored *adj. You look really bored.* jaded, tired, uninterested, weary *****excited**

boring *adj. I found the movie boring and too long.* dreary, dull, humdrum, monotonous, tedious, tiresome *****enjoyable**

borrow *v. Can I borrow a pen?* have, have the loan of, obtain, take temporarily, use *****lend**

boss *n. He hopes to be the boss one day.* chief, director, head, manager, principal, top dog (*informal*)

bossy *adj. My sister is so bossy.* arrogant, authoritarian, domineering, overbearing

bother *v. Does the noise bother you?* annoy, concern, distress, disturb, inconvenience, trouble, worry

bounce *v. The toy bird bounces up and down.* bound, jump, leap, prance, spring

bound *adj. Hayley's so good that she's bound to win.* certain, likely, sure

box *n. We packed all of our belongings in boxes.* carton, case, chest, crate

brave *adj. She was a very brave soldier.* bold, courageous, daring, fearless, heroic *****cowardly**

break[1] *n. Should we stop for a break now?* intermission, interval,

Bridges

Bascule bridge
Drawbridge
Footbridge

Rope bridge
Swing span bridge
Viaduct

Cantilever

Suspension

Beam

Arch

pause, recess, breather (*informal*)

break[2] *v. Dad broke one of our best plates.* crack, fracture, shatter, smash, snap ***repair**

breathe *v. He was breathing deeply.* gasp, gulp, inhale and exhale, pant, wheeze, respire (*formal*)

brief *adj. He gave me a brief account of what happened.* concise, crisp, cursory, short, succinct ***long**

bright *adj. It was a beautiful, bright day.* clear, cloudless, fair, fine, sunny ***dull**
I love bright colors. bold, brilliant, dazzling, intense, radiant, vivid ***pale**
Krishan is a bright boy. able, brilliant, clever, gifted, intelligent, smart, brainy (*informal*)

brilliant *adj. Jill is a brilliant student.* clever, excellent, gifted, outstanding
I noticed a brilliant light in the sky. bright, dazzling, glaring, shining, vivid ***dark**

bring *v. I'll bring you some flowers.* carry, convey, deliver, fetch

bring about *v. The war brought about many changes.* achieve, cause, engender, give rise to, lead to, make happen

bring up *v. He was brought up in Kenya.* educate, nurture, raise, rear

I will bring up that subject at the meeting. bring forth, initiate, raise

brisk *adj. I feel like taking a brisk walk.* bracing, energetic, invigorating ***slow**

broad *adj. The university has a broad range of subjects from which to choose.* comprehensive, extensive, large, vast, wide ***narrow**

build *v. They're going to build a house here.* assemble, construct, erect, put up ***knock down**

build up *v. The investors built up thousands of dollars in different accounts.* accrue, accumulate, amass, collect, gather
The Romans built up their empire for hundreds of years. develop, foster, grow

bulky *adj. This sofa is very bulky.* awkward, big, cumbersome, large, unmanageable, unwieldy ***small**

bully[1] *n. Nobody likes a bully.* intimidator, thug, tormentor, tyrant, bruiser (*informal*)

bully[2] *v. She was severely punished by the school for bullying other children.* harass, intimidate, oppress, terrorize, torment

bump *v. The supermarket cart bumped into a big pile of cans.* collide with, hit, knock into, plow into, strike

bunch *n. I bought a bunch of*

bananas. batch, bundle, clump, cluster, collection

bundle *n. He found a bundle of papers in the drawer.* bunch, heap, mass, package, stack

burn *v. The fire was burning brightly.* be on fire, blaze, flare, flicker, glow
I left the meat in the oven too long and burned it. char, incinerate, scorch, singe

burst *v. The balloon burst.* break open, crack, explode, rupture, shatter, split open

bury *v. They buried the body rather than cremating it.* conceal, cover up, hide, inter, lay to rest, entomb (*formal*)

business *n. A tailor's business is making clothes.* career, job, livelihood, occupation, profession
A business in the city can succeed. company, corporation, enterprise, firm, organization
That's none of your business. affair, concern, problem, responsibility

busy *adj. I can't talk now; I'm busy.* active, occupied, preoccupied, tied up (*informal*) *free
The streets are usually busy in the evening. bustling, buzzing, lively, vibrant *quiet

but *conj. I tried very hard, but I still couldn't do it.* despite that, even so, however, in spite of that, nevertheless, nonetheless, still, yet

buy *v. What did you buy at the store today?* acquire, obtain, procure, purchase *sell

Cc

cabin *n. A little cabin in the mountains is a perfect getaway.* chalet, cottage, hut, shack

café *n. We had a bite to eat in the café.* cafeteria, coffee shop, restaurant, snack bar

call *v. We heard a voice calling in the distance.* cry, cry out, shout, yell
I'll call you tomorrow. give a ring, telephone

calm[1] *v. The teacher tried to calm Melanie after her fall.* comfort, pacify, soothe *upset

calm[2] *adj. The president remained calm throughout the conference.* collected, composed, cool, placid, relaxed *excited

cancel *v. The game had to be canceled.* abandon, abort, call off, postpone *arrange

capable *adj. You're all very capable students.* able, accomplished, competent, skillful, talented

capture *v. The police captured the thief* apprehend, arrest, catch, take into custody, nab (*informal*) *release

care[1] *n. Handle with care!*
attention, caution, heed

care[2] *v. She doesn't care about the grades she gets.* be concerned, bother, mind, worry

care for *v. The staff at the hospital cared for my granddad very well.* attend to, look after, nurse, take care of, tend ***neglect**
She doesn't care for spinach. choose, like, prefer

careful *adj. Be careful when you cross the street.* alert, attentive, cautious, heedful, prudent, wary, watchful ***careless**
My uncle is a very careful driver. accurate, attentive, cautious, conscientious ***careless**

careless *adj. You'd make fewer mistakes if you were not so careless.* inaccurate, inattentive, neglectful, negligent, slapdash, sloppy, thoughtless ***careful**

carelessness *n. The accident was caused by the carelessness of the van driver.* inaccuracy, inattention, negligence, sloppiness, thoughtlessness ***care**

carry *v. I carried the heavy bags myself.* bear, bring, convey, lift, transport, lug (*informal*)

carry on *v. We'll carry on after the break since the bell is just about to ring.* continue, go on, persevere, persist ***stop**

carry out *v. Students should carry out this activity in groups.* achieve, conduct, do, fulfill, implement, perform

case *n. He stored his belongings in a case.* bag, box, chest, container, suitcase, trunk
The newspapers have reported another case of road rage. example, incident, instance, occasion, situation

casual *adj. Some students have a very casual attitude toward their work.* easygoing, nonchalant, offhand, relaxed, unconcerned, uninterested ***careful**
She dressed in casual clothes on Fridays at the office. informal, relaxed, sporty ***formal**
I didn't mean to upset you; it was only a casual comment. accidental, random, throwaway, unintentional, unplanned

catch *v. The shopkeeper caught the thief.* apprehend, arrest, capture, seize, take into custody, nab (*informal*)

cause[1] *n. Scientists don't know the cause of the disease.* origin, reason for, root, source
We will fight for the cause of freedom! belief, conviction, right

cause[2] *v. That driver almost caused an accident.* bring about, create, produce, provoke, result in

caution *n. Proceed with caution.* attention, care, prudence, vigilance, watchfulness

cautious *adj. My grandma is a cautious driver.* attentive, careful, prudent, vigilant, wary, watchful ***reckless**

celebrate *v. Many people in the United States hold parties in the street to celebrate Independence Day.* commemorate, honor, mark, observe

center *n. Find the center of the circle.* core, heart, hub, middle, nucleus ***edge**

ceremony *n. You are invited to my graduation ceremony.* rite, ritual, service

certain *adj. Are you certain that it's true?* confident, convinced, positive, satisfied, sure ***doubtful** *A certain person I know loves that television show.* particular, special, specific

chance *n. I don't want to leave anything to chance.* accident, destiny, fate, fortune, hazard, luck *You'll get a chance to bat later.* occasion, opportunity, possibility, turn

change *v. If you don't like the schedule as it stands, we can change it.* adjust, alter, convert, modify, reform, transform ***preserve**

chaos *n. When the teacher returned, she found a scene of chaos.* confusion, disorder, mayhem, pandemonium, turmoil ***order**

character *n. He can't help it;* *it's in his character.* nature, personality, temperament

charge¹ *n. Everyone complains that bank charges are too high.* cost, fee, price

charge² *v. The bull charged.* advance, attack, rush, stampede *He was charged with murder.* accuse of, blame for, indict for, prosecute for, put on trial for

charming *adj. What a charming little girl.* appealing, delightful, endearing, lovely, pleasant ***disgusting**

chase *v. The gang chased him home.* follow, hunt, pursue, run after, track

cheap *adj. Matches are cheap items.* affordable, bargain, budget, inexpensive, low priced, reasonably priced ***expensive** *She is very cheap when it comes to spending money.* frugal, miserly, thrifty ***generous**

cheat *v. The salesman cheated his customers.* defraud, dupe, hoodwink, swindle, trick, fleece (*informal*), rip off (*informal*)

check *v. The security guard checked our luggage.* examine, inspect, monitor, verify

cheer (up) *v. I did my best to cheer her up when she didn't get the job.* comfort, console, encourage, buck up (*informal*) ***upset**

cheerful *adj. Our mailman is always cheerful.* bright, happy, in good spirits, jolly, joyful,

optimistic, upbeat ***miserable**

cherish v. *I cherished my grandmother's necklace.* hold dear, keep fondly, preserve, prize, treasure

chew v. *They sat chewing on caramel.* bite, chomp, eat, gnaw, grind, munch

chief adj. *The chief engineer called the shots.* foremost, leading, main, principal, senior, top ***minor**

child n. *My family didn't have much money when I was a child.* baby, infant, juvenile, youngster, youth, kid (*informal*)

choice n. *I had no choice; I had to take the job.* alternative, decision, option, way out

choke v. *The fumes began to choke me.* smother, stifle, suffocate

choose v. *Choose whichever one you like.* decide on, elect, opt for, pick, select, specify

chop v. *They spent all morning in the forest chopping wood.* cut, hack, hew, lop, sever

citizen n. *We are all citizens of the world.* member, native, resident, subject

claim v. *He claimed that he was innocent.* assert, declare, insist, maintain, state

clean adj. *These clothes are clean.* immaculate, pure, spotless, unsoiled ***dirty**

clear adj. *On a clear day you can see for miles.* bright, cloudless, fair, fine, light ***cloudy**
She left clear instructions on how to use the washer. distinct, explicit, lucid, understandable ***vague**
It's clear that she knew all

Churches and Places of Worship

Cathedral
Chapel
Church
Mosque
Oratory
Pantheon
Synagogue
Temple

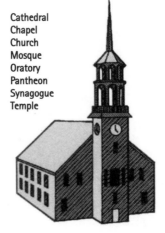

along. apparent, evident, obvious, plain ***uncertain**

climb *v. I love climbing trees.* ascend, go up, mount, scale

clog *v. There's something clogging the sink.* block, jam, obstruct

close¹ *v. (kloze) Close the door, please.* bar, bolt, fasten, secure, shut ***open**

close² *adj. (klose) It's not far from here; in fact, it's really close.* adjacent, near, nearby, neighboring ***far**

cloudy *adj. It was a cloudy day.* dull, gloomy, gray, overcast ***bright**

The liquid in the test tube was

cloudy. muddy, murky, opaque ***clear**

club *n. The mugger was carrying a wooden club.* stick, truncheon
Are you a member of any clubs? association, group, organization, society

clumsy *adj. I'm so clumsy; I'm always dropping things.* awkward, gawky, ungainly

cold *adj. It was a cold day.* bitter, chilly, cool, freezing, frosty, nippy (*informal*) ***hot**
She gave him a cold stare. bitter, glaring, harsh

collapse *v. The building collapsed.* cave in, crumple, fall down,

Clothing

Dresses and trousers	Coats and jackets	Footwear and leg wear	Tops
Bermuda shorts	Blazer	Boots	Blouse
Cocktail dress	Cloak	Galoshes	Cardigan
Evening gown	Parka	Shoes	Shirt
Jeans	Poncho	Slippers	Sweater
Jodhpurs	Raincoat	Sneakers	Sweatshirt
Miniskirt	Suit jacket	Socks	T-shirt
Pants	Tuxedo	Stockings	
Petticoat		Tights	
Sari			
Sarong			
Skirt			

give way, topple

collect v. *I've collected hundreds of rare stamps.* accumulate, amass, assemble, gather, hoard, save

collide v. *The two trucks collided.* crash, meet head-on, smash into

combine v. *Let's combine the letters to make a word.* blend, fuse, join, link, merge, mix, unite *separate

come v. *I'll come over at three o'clock.* appear, arrive, enter, show up *leave

comfortable adj. *This sofa isn't very comfortable.* agreeable, cozy, restful *uncomfortable *I don't feel very comfortable when Mike's around.* at ease, confident, relaxed, laid-back (*informal*) *uncomfortable

comment n. *Do you have any comments to make, Lauren?* observation, opinion, remark, view

common adj. *Nail biting is a common habit among children.* frequent, habitual, widespread *rare

company n. *He works for a big company.* association, business, corporation, enterprise, firm, organization
He enjoys his mother's company. companionship, friendship

competition n. *The tennis competition is on Saturday.* contest, match, tournament

complain v. *They complained about the poor service.* find fault with, grumble, moan, protest, gripe (*informal*), whine (*informal*) *praise

complaint n. *The letter is full of complaints.* criticism, grievance, objection, protest

complete[1] v. *When you've completed question one, go on to question two.* accomplish, end, finish

complete[2] adj. *I've now got a complete set of baseball cards.* entire, full, whole *incomplete

complicated adj. *The application form is complicated.* complex, intricate, involved *clear

compulsory adj. *We have to go to the meeting; it's compulsory.* mandatory, necessary, obligatory, required *optional

conceited adj. *He's so conceited; he thinks he's the best at everything.* arrogant, boastful, egotistical, proud, vain, bigheaded (*informal*), stuck-up (*informal*) *modest

concentrate v. *I want you to concentrate fully on everything I'm telling you.* apply oneself to, focus on, focus one's attention on, heed, pay attention to

concern[1] n. *It's none of my concern.* affair, business, responsibility

concern² *v. It doesn't really concern me.* affect, apply to, be relevant to, involve, relate to

concerned *adj. Mom was concerned when Jenny hadn't called for a few days.* anxious, apprehensive, perturbed, worried *pleased

condition *n. When we bought the house, it was in very good condition.* order, shape, situation, state

confess *v. He confessed that he had stolen the money.* acknowledge, admit, divulge, own up *deny

confident *adj. She always looks so confident when she goes onstage.* fearless, poised, self-assured *shy
I'm confident that we will win the game. certain, positive, sure

confirm *v. All of this only confirms what I have believed for a long time.* attest to, corroborate, endorse, justify, prove, verify *deny

confuse *v. Long words often confuse me.* baffle, bemuse, bewilder, confound, fluster, mystify, perplex, puzzle

connect *v. You need to connect the printer to the computer.* attach, fasten, join, link, unite *disconnect

constant *adj. In this experiment, heat is produced at a constant rate.* consistent, continuous, stable, unchanging, uniform

contact¹ *n. Doctors want to know who has been in contact with the sick person.* association, communication, connection, touch

contact² *v. I'll contact you tomorrow about the tickets.* be in touch with, call, notify, speak to

contain *v. This booklet contains all of the instructions for setting up your computer.* comprise, consist of, hold, include
She tried to contain her anger. control, hold in, suppress

contempt *n. He showed contempt for the audience.* derision, disdain, disrespect, scorn *respect

contest¹ *n. (kon-test) Our best team is taking part in the swimming contest on Saturday.* competition, game, tournament

contest² *v. (kun-test) I will contest this parking ticket.* argue, challenge, dispute

continue *v. Discussions continued throughout the night at the White House.* carry on, go on, keep on, last, persist, proceed *pause

control *v. New Zealand controls some islands in the South Pacific.* administer, command, direct, govern, lead, manage, oversee

convenient *adj. Would Saturday morning be convenient?* appropriate, fit, fitting, suitable

Cooking Utensils

Blender	Griddle	Rolling pin
Bottle	Grill	Saucepan
Bowl	Jar	Sieve
Casserole	Ladle	Skillet
Colander	Lemon squeezer	Spatula
Cup	Masher	Spoon
Cutting board	Measuring cup	Tureen
Dish	Pan	Urn
Food processor	Peeler	Waffle iron
Frying pan	Plate	Whisk
Funnel	Pot	Wok
Grater	Ramekin	

conversation *n. Excuse me, could I interrupt your conversation?* chat, discourse, discussion, exchange, talk

convince *v. He convinced me that it was a good idea.* assure, persuade, prove to, reassure, win over

cool *adj. It feels cool today.* bracing, chilly, cold, nippy (*informal*) *warm
She manages to stay cool even when everyone else is panicking. calm, collected, composed, relaxed, unruffled, laid-back

(*informal*) *excited

cooperate *v. The demonstrators at the peace protest refused to cooperate with the police.* collaborate with, help, join forces with, work with

cope *v. I'm finding it difficult to cope with all of this work.* deal with, grapple with, handle, manage, tackle

copy *v. He watches what people do and then copies them.* ape, imitate, mimic

correct[1] *adj. Yes, that's the correct answer.* accurate, exact, precise, right, true *wrong

correct[2] *v. Let me correct my mistakes.* amend, change, make right, modify

corrupt *adj. They discovered that some agents were corrupt.* dishonest, fraudulent, unscrupulous, crooked (*informal*) *honest

cost *n. The cost is $17.* amount, charge, price

count *v. We need to count how many books there are in the library.* add up, calculate, tally

country *n. There are almost 200 countries in the world.* nation, state, realm (*formal*)

courage *n. The soldiers display a lot of courage when they go into battle.* bravery, daring, fortitude, gallantry, heroism, mettle, pluck, valor, guts (*informal*) *fear

courageous *adj. The award was presented to several courageous children.* bold, brave, fearless, heroic, plucky, valiant *cowardly

cover *v. He covered his face with a scarf so that no one could see his scars.* conceal, hide, mask, obscure, veil *reveal

cowardly *adj. That was mean and cowardly behavior.* fearful, feeble, spineless, timid, weak, wimpish (*informal*) *courageous

crafty *adj. Foxes are said to be crafty creatures.* artful, cunning, shrewd, sly, wily *honest

cram *v. I crammed everything into one drawer.* press, push, ram, squeeze, stuff

crash[1] *n. I heard a loud crash.* bang, clash, clatter, thud

crash[2] *v. The car crashed into a tree and then a wall.* bang into, collide with, hit, plow into, ram into, strike

crawl *v. The children crawled on their hands and knees through the long grass.* creep, slither, squirm, wiggle, worm

crazy *adj. That's a crazy idea!* absurd, idiotic, insane, silly *sensible

creature *n. What's the largest creature in the world?* animal, beast, being, organism

crime *n. He went to prison for his crimes.* fault, misdeed, offense, violation, wrongdoing

crisis *n. A financial crisis is looming.* calamity, catastrophe, disaster, drama

crisp *adj. These cookies are really crisp.* brittle, crispy, crumbly, crunchy, crusty, firm *soft

critical *adj. The journalist wrote a critical article about the president.* censorious, disapproving, fault-finding, judgmental, scathing
Discussions about a pay raise for key workers have reached a critical point. all-important,

Creature

It was a huge beast—the biggest crocodile I'd ever seen.

crucial, decisive, key

criticize *v. Staff criticized the new rules, saying that they would not work.* attack, censure, condemn, denounce, disapprove of, find fault with ***praise**

crooked *adj. This cord is crooked.* bent, bowed, distorted, twisted, warped ***straight**

crouch *v. Charlie crouched down behind the bush.* bow, squat, stoop

crowd *n. A large crowd was blocking the road.* assembly, gathering, horde, mob, multitude, throng

crowded *adj. Buses get very crowded at peak times.* congested, crammed, full, packed, jam-packed (*informal*)

cruel *adj. You shouldn't be cruel to animals.* brutal, callous, inhuman, mean, merciless, ruthless, savage, unkind ***kind**

crush *v. You need to crush the garlic before you put it into the pan.* compress, mash, pound, squash, squeeze

cry *v. "Come here!" she cried.* call, exclaim, shout, shriek, yell *The baby started crying because her diaper needed to be changed.* bawl, shed tears, sob, weep, whimper, blubber (*informal*)

cuddle *v. The baby cried, so his*

mother cuddled him. embrace, fondle, hold, hug

cunning *adj. I've got a cunning plan.* artful, clever, crafty, ingenious, sly, wily, sneaky (*informal*)

cure[1] *n. Doctors haven't discovered a cure for diabetes.* antidote, remedy, treatment

cure[2] *v. A course of antibiotics can be used to cure people with some diseases.* heal, remedy, restore to health, treat

curious *adj. I heard a curious story yesterday.* bizarre, odd, peculiar, strange, unusual, weird *ordinary
Toddlers are instinctively curious about the world.* inquiring, inquisitive, interested, prying, nosy (*informal*)

curl *v. The smoke curled up from the fire and around our heads.* coil, curve, spiral, swirl, twist, wind

current *adj. The current situation looks positive.* contemporary, latest, present, topical *former

custom *n. Decorating a tree is a Christmas custom.* convention, fashion, habit, practice, rite, ritual, tradition

customer *n. There aren't that many customers in the store at the moment.* buyer, client, consumer, patron, purchaser, shopper

cut *v. I cut my finger while I was chopping vegetables.* gash, graze, lacerate, slash, slit, wound
Could you cut me some ham, please? carve, chop, slice

cute *adj. That's a really cute dress.* adorable, appealing, charming, dainty, precious, pretty, sweet

cut off *v. Water supplies to the village have been cut off for a number of days now.* disconnect, interrupt, stop, suspend *connect

Dd

damage[1] *n. Was any serious damage done to the car in the accident?* harm, hurt, injury

damage[2] *v. The vandals damaged the car's paint.* deface, harm, mar, ruin, spoil *repair

damp *adj. The clothes on the line are still a little damp.* moist, soggy, wet *dry
The cottage was cold and damp because it had not been lived in for a long time.* clammy, dank, humid, musty *dry

danger *n. War reporters face great danger daily.* hazard, jeopardy, peril, risk *safety

dangerous *adj. The roads around here are known to be very dangerous for pedestrians.* hazardous, perilous, risky, treacherous, unsafe,

Dances

Ballet	Minuet
Bolero	Polka
Bop	Polonaise
Cha-cha	Quadrille
Charleston	Quickstep
Conga	Rumba
Disco	Salsa
Fandango	Samba
Flamenco	Square dance
Fox trot	Tango
Jitterbug	Tap
Jive	Tarantella
Line dance	Twist
Mazurka	Two-step
Merengue	Waltz

hairy (*informal*) ***safe**

dangle *v. All kinds of charms dangled from the bracelet.* hang, sway, swing

dare *v. No one dared move.* be plucky, have the courage, risk, venture

Go on, I dare you! challenge, defy, provoke

daring *adj. In most fairy tales it is the daring hero who rescues the princess.* adventurous, bold, brave, dashing, fearless ***cowardly**

dark *adj. It's dark in here; turn on the light.* dim, dingy, gloomy, pitch-black, shadowy ***light**

dash *v. Sorry, I must dash; I'm late.* hurry, run, rush, fly (*informal*), get a move on (*informal*) ***dawdle**

dawdle *v. Hurry up! Don't dawdle!* dally, lag behind, linger, loiter, waste time, dilly-dally (*informal*), hang around (*informal*) ***hurry**

dawn *n. The farmer started work at dawn.* daybreak, daylight, first light, morning, sunrise ***dusk**

dead *adj. My grandparents are both dead.* deceased, departed, gone, late, passed away

deadly *adj. A deadly disease threatened the town.* fatal, lethal, life-threatening, mortal

deal¹ *n. They shook hands to seal the deal.* agreement, bargain, compromise, settlement

deal² *v. My uncle used to deal fine art.* buy and sell, market, trade in, traffic in

Rhiannon deals with the general public in her job. attend to, be concerned with, cope with, handle

dear *adj. He's one of my dearest friends.* beloved, cherished, darling, loved, precious

decay[1] *n. Some areas across the country are suffering from neglect and decay.* collapse, decline, deterioration

decay[2] *v. The house's frame was beginning to decay.* decompose, rot

deceive *v. We were all deceived by the letter.* cheat, dupe, fool, hoodwink, mislead, con (*informal*)

decent *adj. Everyone in the world should be able to have a decent standard of living.* adequate, appropriate, fair, proper, reasonable, respectable

decide *v. I can't decide which book to read first.* come to a decision, determine, judge, make up one's mind, reach a decision, resolve

decline *v. Profits in our chain of stores have declined in recent months.* decrease, deteriorate, diminish, drop, dwindle, fall, go down, reduce, sink *increase

She declined my offer to stay for dinner. refuse, reject, turn down

decorate *v. All of the children in the school helped decorate the Christmas tree.* adorn, embellish, garnish, trim

decrease *v. Sales have decreased in the past two months.* decline, deteriorate, diminish, drop, dwindle, fall, go down, reduce, sink *increase

deed *n. He was praised by his teachers for his good deeds.* act, action, exploit, feat

deep *adj. The river is very deep here.* bottomless, extensive, low

If you spoil her things, you'll be in deep trouble. great, intense, profound

defeat *v. They defeated the enemy.* beat, conquer, overcome, overthrow, overwhelm, triumph over, vanquish

defend *v. The army was defending the town from invaders.* fortify, guard, protect, support, uphold *attack

definite *adj. Could you please give me a definite answer?* clear, clear-cut, exact, specific *vague

delay *v. We were delayed by poor weather and heavy traffic.* detain, halt, hinder, hold up, impede

deliberate *adj. He admitted that he had told a deliberate lie.* calculated, intentional, planned, willful

delicate *adj. Be careful with that; it's very delicate.* dainty, fine, flimsy, fragile *strong

delicious *adj. That was a delicious meal.* appetizing, luscious, mouthwatering, tasty,

scrumptious (*informal*),
yummy (*informal*) ***unpleasant**

delight *n. She beamed with delight.* bliss, enjoyment, glee, happiness, joy, pleasure, rapture

delighted *adj. I was absolutely delighted to receive your e-mail.* ecstatic, overjoyed, pleased, thrilled, on cloud nine (*informal*) ***disappointed**

delightful *adj. I had an absolutely delightful time.* agreeable, enchanting, enjoyable, lovely, pleasant, wonderful ***horrible**

deliver *v. The company delivers locally.* carry, convey, drop off, transport

demand *v. The victims demanded answers after the accident.* appeal for, ask for, call for, request

den *n. The animal disappeared inside its den.* burrow, cave, haunt, hideout, lair, nest, shelter

deny *v. She denied that she had been there at the time of the crime.* contradict, refuse, refute, reject, repudiate ***admit**

depart *v. What time does the train depart on Sunday afternoons?* go, leave, quit, retreat, withdraw ***arrive**

department *n. Sally and Rahana work in the same department of the store.* branch, division, section

depend on *v. I'll do it; you can always depend on me.* bank on, count on, have faith in, rely on, trust in

depressed *adj. All of this bad weather makes me feel very depressed.* despondent, disheartened, dispirited, downhearted, low, sad, blue (*informal*) ***cheerful**

describe *v. Can you describe what the thief was wearing?* depict, give a description of, illustrate, portray
Could you please describe clearly what happened? define, detail, explain, give an account of, recount, relate, tell

deserted *adj. The house is deserted.* abandoned, empty, neglected, unoccupied, vacant ***crowded**

deserve *v. You've worked so hard; you deserve a medal.* be entitled to, be worthy of, earn, merit, warrant

design[1] *n. This is the brand-new design for the kitchen.* blueprint, drawing, pattern, plan

design[2] *v. I will design my own skirt.* create, make, plan, style

despair *n. Many people feel a sense of despair when they see pictures of starving children.* depression, distress, gloom, hopelessness, misery, sorrow ***hope**

desperate *adj. She felt so*

desperate *that she ran away
from home.* distraught,
distressed, hopeless, at one's
wits' end (*informal*) *****hopeful**
*Some schools have taken desperate
measures to deal with the problem.*
drastic, extreme, urgent

despite *prep. We had a good time
at the park despite the rain.* in
spite of, regardless of

destroy *v. Vandals broke into
the museum garden and
destroyed the statue.* demolish,
ruin, smash, spoil, wreck
*****build**

destruction *n. Reporters filmed
the scene of destruction caused
by the hurricane.* damage,
desolation, devastation, ruin

detach *v. After use, detach the
earphones from the CD player.*
disconnect, loosen, separate,
undo *****attach**

determined *adj. She was
determined to find out who had
told the teacher about her bad
behavior.* intent on, resolved,
set on, single-minded

develop *v. I'm happy with the way
my career has developed over the
past few years.* evolve, expand,
grow, mature, spread

devote *v. I'm afraid I can't find
any more time to devote to this
project.* allocate, allot, assign,
dedicate, give

devoted *adj. There are many
devoted fans of the Harry Potter
books all over the world.* ardent,
dedicated, devout, loyal,
passionate, staunch *****unfaithful**

diagram *n. Please label the
diagram.* chart, drawing,
illustration, picture, sketch

die *v. Many people of all
nationalities died during the war.*
cease to exist, expire, pass away,
perish *****live**

difference *n. What's the main
difference between a parrot
and a parakeet?* contrast,
discrepancy, dissimilarity,
variation

different *adj. The twins are so
different in character.* contrary,
dissimilar, distinct, distinctive,
diverse, unalike *****same**

difficult *adj. This is a really
difficult equation.* baffling,
challenging, complicated,
demanding, hard, puzzling,
tough, thorny (*informal*) *****easy**
*Please stop being difficult and
start acting your age.*
disobedient, uncooperative

difficulty *n. I had a lot of
difficulty getting through on the
phone.* complication, problem,
trouble

dim *adj. The room was quite dim.*
dark, gloomy, somber, unlit
*****bright**
The lights were dim. faint,
feeble, muted, pale, soft, weak
*****bright**

direct¹ *v. Could you direct me to*

the *restroom, please?* guide, indicate the way, lead, point out, show the way

direct[2] *adj. We'll take the most direct route.* quick, short, straight

directions *n. pl. Read the directions before you turn on the TV.* advice, guidelines, information, instructions, recommendations

dirty *adj. My shoes are dirty.* filthy, grimy, soiled, unclean, grubby (*informal*) ***clean**

disadvantage *n. There are a number of disadvantages to living in the country.* downside, drawback, inconvenience, obstacle ***advantage**

disagree *v. My brother and I disagree about most things.* contrast, differ, have different views, vary ***agree**
I disagree with the action that the committee has taken. disapprove of, object to, oppose, take issue with

disappear *v. The magician made the rabbit disappear.* depart, evaporate, fade away, vanish ***appear**

disappointed *adj. My father was always disappointed with my grades.* dismayed, dissatisfied, frustrated, let down ***pleased**

disapprove *v. The principal disapproves of sneakers.* criticize, denounce, dislike,

frown on (*informal*) ***approve**

disaster *n. There's been a terrible disaster in Italy—an earthquake.* accident, calamity, catastrophe, tragedy

disconnect *v. You should disconnect the cable from the battery before starting the car.* detach, separate, undo, unfasten ***connect**

discover *v. Police have discovered the body of the missing person.* come across, find, locate, unearth ***hide**
I discovered the reason that I have red hair: my mom has red hair too. find out, realize, uncover, unearth

discuss *v. The teachers met to discuss the new school schedule.* confer about, consider, debate, talk over

disgrace *n. His behavior has brought disgrace to the whole school.* dishonor, scandal, shame, stigma

disgusting *adj. The kitchens were so disgusting that there were rats everywhere.* nauseating, repulsive, revolting, sickening, vile ***charming**

dishonest *adj. The dishonest storeowner had been cheating his loyal customers for years.* deceitful, dishonorable, unscrupulous, crooked (*informal*), shady (*informal*) ***honest**

dislike *v. Please tell us if there is*

anything that you dislike about our website. despise, detest, disapprove of, hate, loathe, object to ***like**

disobey *v. Soldiers can be severely punished by the army if they disobey orders.* defy, disregard, ignore, rebel against, violate ***obey**

display *v. The youngest children's work is displayed in the main hall.* exhibit, expose, present, set out, show, unfold ***hide**

district *n. This is the main industrial district of the city.* area, community, county, locality, neighborhood, quarter, region, zone

disturb *v. Please don't disturb me; I'm busy.* annoy, bother, disrupt, interrupt, trouble

dive *v. The bird dived down to the edge of the water and drank.* descend, drop, plummet, plunge, swoop

divide *v. Should we divide the cake into four portions?* apportion, dissect, distribute, split ***join**

do *v. I'm going to do my homework now.* accomplish, carry out, execute, undertake *There's no juice to drink; will water do?* be acceptable, be

Dogs

Afghan hound	Chow	Great Dane	Poodle
Airedale	Collie	Greyhound	Pug
Basset hound	Dachshund	Irish setter	Saint Bernard
Beagle	Dalmatian	Labrador retriever	Spaniel
Bloodhound	Doberman pinscher	Old English	Terrier
Boxer	Foxhound	sheepdog	Whippet
Bulldog	German shepherd	Pekingese	
Chihuahua	Golden retriever	Pointer	

adequate, serve the purpose, suffice, be okay (*informal*)

dodge *v. The senator tried to dodge the questions asked by the press.* avoid, elude, evade, sidestep ***answer**

dog *n. Please walk the dog.* canine, hound, mongrel, mutt, puppy

door *n. The door to the palace was gold.* doorway, entrance, gate, gateway, portal

doubt *v. I've got no reason to doubt the story published in yesterday's paper.* disbelieve, distrust, mistrust, question, suspect ***trust**

doubtful *adj. I have to say that I'm doubtful about the existence of life on other planets.* dubious, skeptical, suspicious, uncertain ***certain**

drag *v. He dragged his suitcase through the station.* haul, pull, tow, tug, lug (*informal*)

drastic *adj. Drastic action on climate change is needed now.* desperate, extreme, harsh, radical, severe ***mild**

draw *v. I'll draw you a picture.* depict, draft, outline, portray, sketch

dread¹ *n. He looked down the dark alley with dread.* fear, terror

dread² *v. I dread walking down that dark street.* be afraid of, be frightened of, fear, worry about ***like**

dreadful *adj. What dreadful news about his sick mother!* alarming, appalling, awful, horrible, shocking, terrible ***mild**

drift *v. The boat drifted farther and farther out to sea.* be

Domesticated Animals

Camel	Goat
Canary	Goose
Cat	Horse
Chicken	Parrot
Cow	Pig
Dog	Pigeon
Donkey	Rabbit
Duck	Sheep

carried, bob, float, glide,
meander, stray

drink v. *She always drank her tea from a china cup.* gulp, sip, swallow, guzzle (*informal*), imbibe (*formal*), quaff (*old-fashioned*)

drip v. *Oil dripped slowly from the can.* drizzle, ooze, seep, trickle

drive v. *I'd love to learn how to drive a tractor.* guide, handle, operate, steer

drop[1] n. *Little drops of dew had formed on the petals in the early morning.* bead, droplet, globule, spot

drop[2] v. *Martha dropped the plate.* let fall, let go of
The temperature on the mountain had dropped sharply overnight. dip, fall, plummet, plunge, sink ***rise**
The town council has dropped its plans to close the hospital. abandon, cancel, forgo, give up, stop ***preserve**

dry adj. *The Sahara desert is an extremely dry region of the world; there is hardly any water there.* arid, dehydrated, dried up, moistureless, parched ***wet**

due adj. *What time do you think the plane is due to arrive?* anticipated, expected, scheduled
The rent for my apartment is due tomorrow. outstanding, owed, owing, payable
With all due respect, I must

disagree. appropriate, correct, fitting, proper ***inappropriate**

dull adj. *Tuesday was a very dull, cold, and rainy day.* cloudy, dim, gloomy, gray, overcast
*bright
I'm tired of wearing clothes in dull colors. drab, dreary, nondescript, somber
*bright
This is an extremely dull, badly written book. boring, dry, humdrum, monotonous, tedious, uninteresting
*interesting

dump v. *He dumped his bag on the chair.* deposit, lay down, put down, plunk (*informal*)
If you don't want it, dump it. discard, dispose of, get rid of, scrap, throw away, ditch (*informal*)

dusk n. *I hope to get home before dusk.* evening, nightfall, sunset, twilight ***dawn**

duty n. *I felt it was my duty to stay with him while we waited for the doctor.* job, obligation, responsibility, task

Ee

eager adj. *Eager fans waited all day.* anxious, ardent, avid, enthusiastic, keen, zealous
*bored

early *adv. We're early; there's no one else here yet.* ahead of time, before time, in advance, in good time, too soon ***late**

earn *v. I earn a lot less than my sister.* be paid, get, make, receive, take home ***spend**
Luke has earned the respect of all of his classmates. deserve, gain, merit, win ***lose**

earth *n. The blue whale is the biggest creature on Earth.* globe, planet, world
Worms wiggle through earth. dirt, ground, soil

easy *adj. The test was very easy.* basic, elementary, simple, straightforward, undemanding, a piece of cake (*informal*) ***difficult**

eat *v. I'll come after I've eaten my lunch.* consume, have, swallow.
He ate his meal quickly. devour, gobble, gulp, polish off (*informal*), wolf down (*informal*)
She will eat only a tiny amount of her meal. nibble, peck at, pick at

economical *adj. Lasagna is an economical family meal.* cheap, inexpensive, reasonable ***expensive**
My granny has always been an economical shopper. careful, frugal, thrifty ***extravagant**

edge *n. The swimming pool is situated on the edge of town.* boundary, fringe, margin, outskirts

educated *adj. Canada has a highly educated, skilled population.* cultured, erudite, informed, learned, literate, well-read ***ignorant**

effect *n. What are the causes and effects of stress?* consequence, end result, impact, outcome, result

effective *adj. Effective study skills produce good results.* productive, successful, useful ***useless**

Eating and Drinking Verbs

Breakfast	Partake, peck at, pick at
Chew, chomp, consume	Quaff
Devour, dig in, dine, drink	Relish
Eat, eat up	Sample, savor, sip, slurp,
Feast, feed, finish off	snack, sup, swallow, swig,
Gobble, gorge, gulp, guzzle	swill
Imbibe	Taste
Lap up, lunch	Wash down, wine and dine,
Masticate, munch	wolf down
Nibble, nosh	

efficient *adj. An efficient public transportation system is needed in every large city.* effective, orderly, well organized, well run ***inefficient**
She's very efficient at her job. able, competent, effective, productive, proficient ***inefficient**

effort *n. The teachers put in a lot of effort to make sure that the event went well.* application, exertion, labor, toil, work

elect *v. The club has elected a new president.* appoint, choose, pick, select, vote in

elegant *adj. You're looking very elegant today, Miranda.* classy, graceful, polished, refined, sophisticated, stylish ***scruffy**

embarrass *v. My parents embarrassed me in front of my friends.* humiliate, mortify, shame

embarrassed *adj. I always feel so embarrassed onstage.* ashamed, awkward, self-conscious, shy, uncomfortable, red-faced (*informal*) ***confident**

emerge *v. The suspect emerged from the building with his hands up in the air.* appear, come into view, come out, exit ***enter**
It emerged that the government had known the truth all along. become known, be revealed, come to light, transpire

emergency *n. In an emergency,* *don't use the elevator.* crisis, extremity, plight, predicament, urgent situation

emotion *n. She never shows her true emotions.* feeling, sentiment
He couldn't speak; he was so overcome by emotion. ardor, fervor, passion

emotional *adj. The parents of the missing child made an emotional appeal on television.* moving, poignant, touching
Some people get very emotional on the subject. excitable, fervent, passionate

emphasize *v. Business leaders emphasize the importance of knowing foreign languages.* accent, accentuate, highlight, stress, underline

employ *v. They employ my father to deliver pizzas.* engage, hire, recruit, retain, use

empty *adj. The house at the end of the street has been empty for months.* bare, deserted, uninhabited, unoccupied, vacant

encourage *v. We were encouraged by the news from the hospital.* cheer, hearten, support, uplift
Joshua's parents encouraged him to take karate. inspire, persuade, prompt, urge

end¹ *n. The end of the story made me cry.* close, conclusion, ending, finale, finish ***start**
My house is at the end of the

street. boundary, edge, extremity, limit

end² *v. We'll end the class now.* break off, close, finish, stop, terminate *****start**

endless *adj. The summer seemed endless.* ceaseless, continual, continuous, everlasting, limitless *****short**

I'm fed up with endless shows about celebrities. countless, numerous, repeated, untold *****few**

enemy *n. The current president has many enemies.* adversary, antagonist, foe, opponent, rival *****friend**

energetic *adj. She leads a very busy and energetic lifestyle.* active, dynamic, lively, vibrant *****lazy** *Skiing is an energetic sport.* demanding, strenuous, vigorous *****gentle**

energy *n. If you ate more healthily, you'd have more energy.* force, power, stamina, vigor, vitality

enjoy *v. My dad enjoys cooking.* appreciate, be fond of, delight in, like, relish *****dislike**

enjoyable *adj. I had an enjoyable evening at the theater.* agreeable, amusing, delightful, entertaining, likable, pleasant *****boring**

enormous *adj. What an enormous monster!* colossal, gigantic, huge, immense, massive, vast *****tiny**

enough¹ *adj. There's enough food*

Engines

Diesel engine
Internal combustion engine
Jet engine
Piston engine
Steam engine
Turbojet engine
Turboprop engine

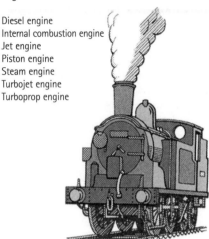

here to feed an army. adequate, ample, plenty, sufficient

enough² *adv. Did she practice her guitar enough for today?* fully, sufficiently

enter *v. He entered the room without knocking.* barge into, burst into, come in, gain access to, go in, make an entrance, set foot in *****leave**

entertain *v. The clown entertained the children.* amuse, charm, delight, please

enthusiasm *n. It's great to see such enthusiasm on the football field.* ardor, eagerness, fervor, passion, zeal, zest

enthusiastic *adj. Nadia is very enthusiastic about her new job.* animated, ardent, eager, excited,

passionate, zealous ***bored**
entire *adj. Is that the entire story?*
complete, full, total, whole
envious *adj. I feel a little envious*
that she's going to the concert.
begrudging, jealous, resentful
*pleased
environment *n. I really can't study*
in a noisy environment.
atmosphere, background,
conditions, situation,
surroundings
envy *v. I don't envy you having to*
take two buses to school.
begrudge, be jealous of, resent
episode *n. The series consists of*
four episodes. act, chapter,
installment, section
equal *adj. We both work in sales,*
but we don't get equal pay. alike,
equivalent, identical, matching,
same ***different**
equipment *n. We left some of our*
equipment behind. apparatus,
gear, paraphernalia, supplies
equivalent *adj. One dollar is*
equivalent to 100 pennies.
comparable, equal, similar
escape *v. The prisoner escaped*
from jail. bolt, break free, flee,
get away, make a getaway, make
a run for it (*informal*)
I hope to escape my mother's
wrath when she realizes that I
didn't do the dishes. avoid, be
free of, elude
especially *adv. Most fruit,*
especially oranges and other

citrus, contain vitamin C.
chiefly, in particular, mainly,
notably, particularly, principally
essential *adj. It's absolutely*
essential for our success that all
team members attend the
meeting. crucial, necessary,
needed, required, requisite,
vital ***optional**
establish *v. The school was*
established in 1889. create,
form, found, launch, set up
estimate *v. We had to estimate*
the size of the angle. assess,
calculate, gauge
even[1] *adj. An even surface is*
necessary when completing a
puzzle. flat, flush, level, smooth
*uneven
even[2] *adv. There were a lot of*
people at the demonstration
yesterday, but there are even
more today. still, yet
event *n. Award giving is an annual*
event at most schools. function,
happening, incident, occasion,
occurrence
ever *adv. It's the best present I've*
ever received. at any time, until
now, up till now
Studies show that there will be
an ever-increasing number of air
travelers in the future. always,
constantly, endlessly, forever,
perpetually ***never**
evidence *n. What evidence do you*
have that it was Hugo who took
the money? confirmation,

grounds, proof

evil *adj. According to the legend, Snow White's stepmother was evil.* bad, malevolent, sinful, wicked ***good**

exact *adj. What is the exact time?* accurate, correct, precise, right ***approximate**

exaggerate *v. Please don't exaggerate; there aren't as many as that.* amplify, magnify, overestimate, overstate, stretch the truth (*informal*)

examine *v. Police are examining clues found at the scene.* analyze, check, inspect, investigate, scrutinize

example *n. Let me give you an example of what I'm talking about.* case, illustration, instance, sample, specimen

excellent *adj. He produced an excellent piece of work.* exceptional, first-rate, outstanding, superb, wonderful ***poor**

except *prep. Everyone except Jessica was invited to the party.* apart from, barring, besides, excluding, save, with the exception of

excess *n. Obesity means having an excess of body fat.* glut, surfeit, surplus, too much

exchange *v. I'd like to exchange this skirt for a smaller size.* change, convert, swap, trade

excited *adj. I'm so excited to*

be at the circus. delighted, ecstatic, thrilled ***bored**

exciting *adj. The new James Bond movie is an exciting film.* dramatic, exhilarating, gripping, thrilling ***boring**

exclude *v. The club excludes people under the age of 21.* ban, bar, disbar, keep out ***allow**
If you exclude the silly mistakes, this is a really good piece of work. eliminate, forget about, ignore, leave out, rule out ***include**

excuse[1] (*ek-skyoos*) *n. That's still not a valid excuse for this kind of bad behavior.* cause, explanation, grounds, justification, reason

excuse[2] (*ek-skyooz*) *v. The committee excused him for his bad behavior.* absolve, forgive, pardon, let off the hook (*informal*) ***accuse**

exercise[1] *n. This is an exercise in self-control.* act, activity, task

exercise[2] *v. My mom exercises vigorously every day in order to stay in shape.* practice, train, work out
I'm going to exercise my right to free speech. employ, execute, exert, follow through on, practice

exhibition *n. I'm going to see an art exhibition on Saturday at the Met.* display, exposition, fair, show, spectacle

expand v. *The suitcase is able to expand to make room for extra clothes.* enlarge, grow, increase in size, spread, swell

expect v. *I'm expecting a very important delivery today.* anticipate, hope for, look forward to, look out for
I expect you've been invited to Tracy's party. assume, imagine, presume, suppose, guess (*informal*)

expel v. *He was expelled from his last school for often being absent without permission.* bar, dismiss, eject, evict, oust, throw out, kick out (*informal*)
*admit

expensive adj. *He bought a very expensive pair of shoes.* costly, extortionate, highly priced, high priced, pricey (*informal*)
*cheap

experience[1] n. *You need a lot of experience for this job.* knowledge, practice, training, know-how (*informal*)

experience[2] v. *Let's experience everything that the city has to offer.* do, take in, try

experienced adj. *She's an experienced teacher who has worked at the school for many years.* accomplished, expert, knowledgeable, skillful, trained

experiment n. *Scientists carried out a series of experiments.* analysis, check, investigation, test, trial

expert n. *If you want to know, ask an expert.* authority, master, professional, specialist, virtuoso ***beginner**

expire v. *My passport is going to expire next year.* become invalid, come to an end, lapse, run out ***begin**

explain v. *Can you explain why the gas turned purple?* clarify, describe, elucidate, expound, spell out

explanation n. *The textbook gives no explanation as to why French verbs change.* clarification, commentary, description, elucidation, exposition, reason

explode v. *A number of bombs have exploded.* blow up, detonate, go off

explore v. *The children explored the beach.* examine, inspect, investigate, look at, tour

express v. *The teacher's face expressed curiosity.* communicate, demonstrate, show
You must express your ideas clearly if you want to succeed as a writer. articulate, phrase, put into words, say, utter, voice

expression n. *Dictionaries are full of useful expressions.* idiom, phrase, sentence, statement, term
She had a very bored expression

on her face. air, appearance, look, countenance (*literary*)

extra *adj. I need extra time to finish the test.* additional, further, more, supplementary ***less**

extravagant *adj. Since getting a Saturday job, Tammy has become very extravagant.* free spending, lavish, reckless, wasteful, prodigal (*formal*) *****economical**

extreme *adj. The presidential candidate has some extreme views.* excessive, hard-line, outrageous, radical, very strong

Ff

fact *n. The world is getting warmer, and that's a fact.* actuality, reality, truth *****lie**
The website gives plenty of facts about global warming. data, detail, information, point

factory *n. The factory closed last year.* mill, plant, works

fade *v. These jeans have faded.* become bleached, become lighter, discolor, lose color
His voice faded away as he left the stage. dim, dwindle, peter out (*informal*)

fail *v. He failed for the second time.* be unsuccessful, lack success, flop (*informal*) *****succeed**

failure *n. The concert was a complete failure.* disaster, fiasco, flop (*informal*) *****success**

faint¹ *v. He fainted in the heat.* collapse, lose consciousness, pass out, swoon (*literary*)

faint² *adj. After the operation, I was left with a faint scar.* indistinct, pale, slight, unobtrusive *****clear**

fair *adj. Jamie's got a bigger piece—that's not fair.* impartial, just *****unfair**
A means excellent, B good, and C fair. acceptable, average, mediocre, moderate, passable, reasonable, satisfactory
Georgie has fair hair. blond, golden, light, flaxen (*literary*)

fairly *adv. It's a fairly good book.* reasonably, somewhat, pretty (*informal*) *****very**

faith *n. There are children of all faiths in this school.* belief, creed, religion
I don't have any faith in official statistics anymore. belief, confidence, trust

faithful *adj. A faithful friend is hard to find.* constant, loyal, staunch, true, trusted *****unfaithful**

fake *adj. The criminals were selling fake ID cards.* bogus, counterfeit, false, forged, phony (*informal*) *****real**

fall *v. The toddler fell in the park.* keel over, stumble, topple over,

trip, tumble
The price of oil has fallen.
decline, diminish, drop, dwindle, lessen, reduce *rise

fall through v. *Our plans fell through.* collapse, fail, founder *succeed

false adj. *The thief gave a false alibi.* fake, fictitious, flawed, inaccurate, incorrect, untrue, wrong *correct

fame n. *How do celebrities cope with fame?* celebrity, glory, popularity, renown, stardom

familiar adj. *It's nice to see some familiar faces.* common, frequent, recognizable, usual, well-known *unfamiliar

famous adj. *There were lots of famous people at the premiere.* celebrated, eminent, notorious, renowned, well-known *unknown

fan n. *The fans cheered when he scored the touchdown.* admirer, enthusiast, follower, supporter

fancy adj. *Mom bought some fancy cakes.* decorated, decorative, elaborate, ornate *plain

fantastic adj. *It was a fantastic experience.* amazing, excellent, superb, terrific, wonderful *terrible

far adj. *On the far edge of town, there are railroad tracks.* distant, faraway, remote *near

fashion n. *Dresses are not in fashion this season.* craze, style, trend, vogue

fashionable adj. *Denim is fashionable at the moment.* popular, stylish, trendy, up-to-date, all the rage (*informal*), hip (*informal*) *old-fashioned

fast adj. *The fast train to Boston took only one hour.* express, quick, rapid, speedy, swift *slow

fasten v. *The cowboy fastened his horse to a post.* attach, fix, hitch, secure, tether, tie *unfasten

fat adj. *The puppy is very fat.* chubby, corpulent, obese, overweight, plump, portly, stout, tubby (*informal*) *thin

fate n. *I didn't plan it; it was fate that made it happen.* destiny, fortune, providence

fault n. *Please check the goods to see if there are any faults.* defect, flaw, imperfection
Sorry, it was my fault. error, mistake, responsibility

faulty adj. *The hair dryer was faulty, so I got my money back.* broken, defective, imperfect, unsound *perfect

favor[1] n. *Could you please do me a favor?* benefit, courtesy, good turn, service

favor[2] v. *She tends to favor her left foot.* be partial to, give preference to, prefer

favorite adj. *The Rolling Stones is my favorite band of all* *time.* best loved, chosen, preferred

fear *n. The boys showed no signs of fear in the face of danger.* alarm, dread, fright, horror, panic, terror ***courage**

feed *v. The sow was feeding her piglets.* nourish, suckle, sustain

feel *v. Feel how soft this velvet is.* caress, fondle, handle, stroke, touch
I feel I need a vacation soon. be aware, believe, consider, sense, think

feeling *n. Do you think animals have feelings?* emotion, sensibility, sentiment

fence *n. There's a fence around the garden.* barrier, hoarding, paling, railing

festival *n. The annual festival celebrates diversity.* carnival, celebration, fete, gala, jamboree

fetch *v. Could you please fetch me my glasses?* bring, carry, get, reach

few *adj. He has very few friends.* a small number of, hardly any, not many, one or two ***many**
There are still a few cookies left. a handful of, a small number of, several, some ***many**

fidget *v. Sit still! Don't fidget!* be agitated, be jittery, jiggle, squirm, wiggle

field *n. The farm is surrounded by fields.* green, meadow, pasture

fierce *adj. A fierce dog threatened*

him. aggressive, ferocious, savage, wild ***gentle**

fight¹ *v. The men began fighting after the game.* battle, brawl, come to blows, scrap (*informal*)

fight² *n. There was a fight on the playground.* altercation, battle, brawl, conflict, scrap (*informal*)

figure *n. Write down these figures.* character, digit, number, numeral, symbol
She's got a nice figure. build, form, physique, shape
There was a figure in the distance. form, outline, person, shape

file *n. Keep your papers in a file.* binder, case, folder

fill *v. We filled several bags with garbage.* cram, load, pack, stuff (*informal*)

final *adj. The final scene of the play is very sad.* closing, concluding, end, last, ultimate ***first**

find *v. I finally found my watch; it had fallen behind the chair in the living room.* come across, discover, locate, pinpoint, track down, unearth ***lose**

fine¹ *n. He had to pay a large fine of $300.* fee, forfeit, penalty, punishment

fine² *adj. How are you? Fine, thanks.* all right, in good health, well, okay (*informal*) ***sick**
The painting is a fine example of Victorian art. excellent,

Flags

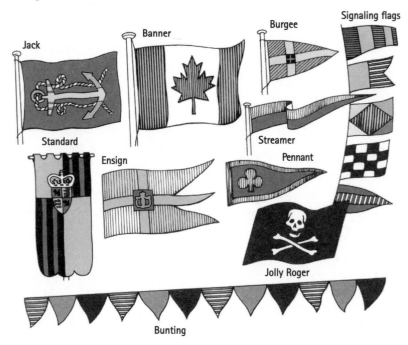

Jack

Banner

Burgee

Signaling flags

Standard

Streamer

Ensign

Pennant

Jolly Roger

Bunting

first-class, first-rate, good,
great (*informal*) *bad*
*If the weather's fine, we'll be
able to have a picnic.* bright,
clear, cloudless, pleasant,
sunny, warm
*Fine particles of rocks and shells
made up the sand.* delicate,
ground, powdery
finish *v. I've almost finished
my homework.* accomplish,
bring to a close, complete,
conclude *begin*
fire *v. Jo was fired from her job.*

discharge, dismiss, lay off
firm[1] *n. My mom works for a
firm that makes water pumps.*
business, company, enterprise,
organization
firm[2] *adj. Put the glass on a
table or other firm surface.*
hard, rigid, solid, stable,
steady, sturdy *soft*
first *adj. The first chapter of
the book is scary.* beginning,
initial, introductory, opening,
preliminary *last*
fit *adj. These old rags aren't*

fit for anything. appropriate, apt, fitting, proper, suitable ***unsuitable**

I try my best to stay fit. healthy, in good condition, in good shape, trim ***unfit**

fix *v. My phone's broken, and it looks as if it will cost a lot of money to fix it.* mend, overhaul, put right, repair, service ***break**

flag *n. The flag is flying.* banner, pennant

flash *v. Lights were flashing.* beam, gleam, glimmer, glitter, shine, sparkle, twinkle

flat *adj. The land is very flat around here.* even, horizontal, level, smooth ***uneven**

flatter *v. You're flattering me only so that I do what you want.* compliment, fawn over, praise, butter up (*informal*), sweet-talk (*informal*) ***insult**

flavor *n. I used herbs to add flavor.* seasoning, tang, taste

flexible *adj. We need a flexible piece of wire.* elastic, malleable, pliable, pliant, supple

flood *v. We were flooded with complaints.* deluge, drown, engulf, inundate, overwhelm, swamp

flow *v. The river flows through the valley.* gush, pour, run, stream, surge, sweep

fly *v. The bird flew over the tops of the trees.* glide, hover, soar, take flight

fog *n. The fog made it difficult to see far ahead.* haze, mist, smog, vapor

foggy *adj. It was a foggy day.* hazy, misty, murky

fold *v. I folded the piece of paper in half.* crease, pleat ***spread**

follow *v. The spy followed the politician all over the city.* chase, go behind, pursue, shadow, tail, trace ***lead**

I couldn't really follow the meaning of what she was saying. comprehend, grasp, take in, understand

fool[1] *n. What a fool I have been!* blockhead, clown, dunce, idiot, simpleton, dope (*informal*)

fool[2] *v. You can't fool me; I'm not a complete idiot.* deceive, hoodwink, mislead, trick, con (*informal*)

foolish *adj. That was a foolish thing to do.* absurd, crazy, ridiculous, silly, unwise ***sensible**

forbid *v. The young offenders are forbidden from leaving their rooms.* ban, bar, outlaw, prohibit ***allow**

force[1] *n. The force of the wind was so strong that it blew the roof off our house.* energy, might, power, strength

force[2] *v. The robbers forced the bank manager to open the safe.* coerce, compel, make, oblige, push

forecast v. *They are forecasting bad weather for tomorrow.* expect, foresee, foretell, predict, prophesy

forge v. *The gang had forged hundreds of passports.* copy, counterfeit, fake, falsify, imitate, pirate

forgery n. *This $20 bill is actually a forgery.* copy, counterfeit, dud, fake, fraud, imitation, sham, phony (*informal*)

forget v. *I've forgotten my bathing suit.* fail to bring, leave at home, leave behind, neglect to bring, overlook ***remember** *I'm sorry, but I forgot your name.* be unable to recall/remember

forgive v. *The victim was able to forgive her attacker.* absolve, excuse, let off, pardon, reprieve ***blame**

form[1] n. *Walking is one of the best forms of exercise you can do.* kind, manner, sort, style, type, variety

form[2] v. *The snowflakes formed a pretty pattern on the glass.* create, fashion, forge, make, produce

formal adj. *Graduation is usually a formal occasion.* ceremonial, ceremonious, dignified, official, solemn ***informal**

former adj. *He's a former student of the school's.* earlier, one-time, previous, prior ***future**

fortunate adj. *It was quite fortunate that there was a doctor on board the plane.* advantageous, auspicious, beneficial, happy, lucky ***unfortunate**

fortune n. *He made a fortune selling all of his old computer equipment on an Internet auction site.* a huge amount, a lot of money, a bomb (*informal*), megabucks (*informal*) *In the past, many poor Europeans went to America to seek their fortune.* affluence, riches, wealth

foundation n. *The course you are taking now will provide an extremely good foundation for the work you'll do in college.* base, basis, groundwork, starting point

fragile adj. *Please be very careful with that vase; it's fragile.* breakable, brittle, delicate, flimsy, frail ***strong**

frantic adj. *Her mother was frantic with worry by midnight.* agitated, distraught, hysterical, panic-stricken, in a state (*informal*) ***calm**

fraud n. *He was jailed for fraud.* cheat, deceit, deception, swindling

free[1] v. *The animal-rights demonstrators freed the chickens from their cages.* emancipate, let loose, liberate, release, unlease ***capture**

free[2] adj. *The animals are running free around the yard.* at large, at liberty, on the loose, unchained, unrestricted *Are you free on Saturday afternoon?* available, off,

unoccupied ***busy**
It doesn't cost anything to
upgrade your phone; it's free.
complimentary, free of charge,
gratis, gratuitous, on the house
(*informal*) ***expensive**

freedom *n. Spartacus demanded*
freedom for the slaves.
emancipation, independence,
liberation, liberty

fresh *adj. You should eat plenty*
of fresh vegetables every day.
natural, recently picked,
unprocessed ***rotten**
We need some fresh air. clean,
cool, invigorating, pure,
refreshing

friend *n. We've been friends for*
years. ally, companion, buddy
(*informal*), chum (*informal*),
crony (*informal*), pal (*informal*)
*enemy

friendly *adj. Our new neighbors*
are extremely friendly. affable,
amiable, convivial, cordial,
genial, sociable ***hostile**

fright *n. I got a fright when the*
mouse ran out. scare, shock,
start

frighten *v. I'm terribly sorry for*
creeping up on you; I didn't
mean to frighten you. alarm,
scare, startle, terrify

frightening *adj. We watched*
a horror movie; it was really
frightening. alarming, scary,
terrifying

front *n. I want to get there very*
early so that I can beat the rush
and be at the front of the line.
beginning, head, lead, start
*back

frown *v. The teacher frowned*
when I showed her the work in
my notebook. glare, glower,
scowl ***smile**

full *adj. The bus is full; get off,*
please. crammed, crowded,
loaded, packed, bursting at the
seams (*informal*), jam-packed
(*informal*) ***empty**

fun *n. We had a lot of fun at the*
circus. amusement, enjoyment,
entertainment, pleasure, sport
(*old-fashioned*)

function[1] *n. The main function*
of the school committee is to
organize the annual concert.
activity, duty, purpose,
responsibility, role, task

function[2] *v. How do the leg*
muscles function? act, behave,
operate, work

fund *n. I always keep a separate*
fund for emergencies. kitty,
pool, reserve, stock, supply

funny *adj. It's a really funny*
movie. amusing, comical, droll,
hilarious, humorous, witty
*serious
There's something funny about
this old box. bizarre, curious,
odd, peculiar, strange, weird

fuss *n. What's all the fuss about?*
ado, bustle, commotion,
excitement, stir, uproar,

hullabaloo (*informal*), to-do (*informal*)

fussy *adj. She's so fussy about keeping her house clean.* fastidious, finicky, exacting, particular, nitpicky (*informal*), persnickety (*informal*)

future *adj. Here's a list of future events to be held at the school.* coming, forthcoming, impending, later ***former**

Gg

gain *v. Volunteers will gain valuable experience.* acquire, attain, benefit from, get, obtain

game *n. This outdoor game is fun for all ages.* activity, amusement, pastime, sport

gap *n. There was a gap in the fence through which you could look.* crack, cranny, hole, opening, slot, space

garbage *n. Take all of your garbage out to the curb.* debris, litter, refuse, trash, waste
The cellar is full of garbage. clutter, junk, odds and ends (*informal*)
Don't talk such garbage. claptrap, gibberish, nonsense, trash, drivel (*informal*), poppycock (*informal*)

gather *v. Gather all of your things together.* amass, assemble, collect, pick up

We were asked to gather in the gym. assemble, congregate, convene, meet ***scatter**
I gather your mom has a new job. be led to believe, believe, understand

gear *n. Don't forget to pack your climbing gear.* apparatus, equipment, paraphernalia

general *adj. The general feeling of the meeting was that he should resign.* common, overall, widespread, across-the-board (*informal*)
Don't worry about the details; just give me the general outlook. approximate, broad, nonspecific, overall

generous *adj. What a lovely present; you are very generous.* benevolent, bighearted, kind, lavish, liberal, magnanimous, unselfish ***stingy**
There was a generous amount of tea and coffee in the hotel room. abundant, ample, liberal, plentiful ***scarce**

gentle *adj. You should be gentle when you play with your baby sister.* kind, mild, soft, tender ***rough**
A gentle breeze blew. faint, light, mild, moderate, pleasant, slight, soft ***strong**

gesture *n. I'll make a gesture when it's time for you to go on the stage.* indication, movement, nod, sign, signal

get *v. I got lots of presents.*

acquire, gain, obtain, receive
*Will you get me a loaf of bread
while you're out?* buy, fetch,
obtain, procure, purchase
It's getting dark. become,
grow, turn
I never get jokes. comprehend,
follow, grasp, understand,
figure out (*informal*)
get rid of *v.* see **rid**
get up *v. I get up early every day.*
rise, stir, wake up, arise (*formal*)
ghost *n. Do you believe in ghosts?*
apparition, phantom, specter,
spirit, spook
gift *n. Thank you for your very
generous gift.* contribution,
donation, present
Samia has a gift for languages.
ability, aptitude, flair, skill, talent
gist *n. Just give me the gist of the
story.* essence, important points,
main points, nub, significance,
substance
give *v. They give a lot of money to
charity.* distribute, donate, grant,
hand over, offer, supply ***accept**
*We pushed hard, and eventually
the lock gave.* bend, break,
collapse, give way, yield
give in *v. He knew he was wrong,
but he wouldn't give in.* admit
defeat, relent, surrender, yield
give out *v. Can you please give
out these papers?* allocate,
distribute, hand out, pass
around, pass out
give up *v. It's very difficult to give*

up smoking. abandon, cease,
discontinue, stop, quit (*informal*)
*start
glad *adj. I'm very glad you called.*
delighted, happy, pleased ***sorry**
gloomy *adj. It was a gloomy room
with very small windows.* cheerless,
dark, dim, dismal, dreary ***bright**
*You're looking very gloomy today,
Becky. Is there anything wrong?*
dejected, depressed, downcast,
glum, miserable, sad, somber,
unhappy, blue (*informal*), down
in the dumps (*informal*)
*cheerful
glossy *adj. The horse had a very
glossy coat.* burnished, gleaming,
polished, shiny, sleek ***dull**
glow *v. I could see lights glowing
in the distance.* gleam, shine,
twinkle
go *v. My mom has gone to the
mall.* move, travel, walk, step
out (*informal*) ***come**
This road goes to the river.
continue, extend, lead, proceed
go by *v. Several hours went by.*
elapse, pass, slip by
good *adj. She saw a good movie.*
excellent, fine, great, outstanding,
wonderful ***bad**
*Lemons are good for colds and
flus.* appropriate, beneficial, fit,
suitable
Cabbage is good for you.
beneficial, healthy, wholesome
*unhealthy
Nathan is good at math. able,

capable, competent, expert, talented

goods *n. pl. These goods are for export.* articles, commodities, items, merchandise, products, wares

go off *v. The bomb went off.* blow up, detonate, explode

go on *v. Go on, I'm listening.* carry on, continue, proceed ***stop**

grab *v. Ben grabbed his bag.* grasp, seize, snatch, take

grade *n. I've completed more than most kids in my grade.* class, level, rank, stage

gradually *adv. He built up his strength gradually.* bit by bit, by degrees, little by little, piece by piece, step by step ***suddenly**

grasp *v. She grasped my hand.* clutch, grab, grip, seize, take hold of
I find the facts about this point very hard to grasp. absorb, assimilate, comprehend, follow, understand

grateful *adj. I'm very grateful for all of your help.* appreciative (of), indebted, obliged, thankful ***ungrateful**

great *adj. The exhibition attracted a great number of visitors.* considerable, large, significant, substantial ***small**
Winston Churchill was a great man. distinguished, eminent, illustrious, important, prominent ***minor**
It was a great movie; we loved it. enjoyable, excellent, fantastic, first-rate, superb, wonderful ***terrible**

greedy *adj. Please don't take all of the cake; that's just greedy.* gluttonous, selfish, voracious ***generous**

green *adj. I bought a pair of green pants.* aqua, emerald,

Groups of Animals

A cete of badgers
A colony ôf seals
A drove of cattle
A flock of birds
A herd of elephants
A mob of kangaroos
A pack of wolves
A pride of lions
A school of porpoises
A skulk of foxes
A sloth of bears
A swarm of bees
A troop of monkeys

jade, olive

The new recruits were still green. immature, inexperienced, naive, raw, untrained ***experienced**

Catherine entered politics because she was very interested in green issues. ecological, environmental

greet *v. Two students greeted visitors on their arrival.* meet, receive, welcome

grief *n. The mourners couldn't hide their grief.* anguish, distress, sadness, sorrow, woe ***happiness**

grieve *v. The widower is still grieving for his wife.* be in mourning, be sad, lament, mourn

grim *adj. Louise sat with folded arms and a grim face.* dour, forbidding, serious, stern ***pleasant**

He lived in grim public housing on the outskirts of the city. dismal, dreary, gloomy, horrible, miserable ***pleasant**

groan *v. He just sat there groaning and muttering.* complain, grumble, moan, murmur, sigh, whine (*informal*)

ground *n. We sat on the ground.* earth, land

grounds *n. pl. The castle grounds are huge.* estate, gardens, parkland

There are reasonable grounds to believe that he committed the crime. argument, basis, cause, foundation, reason

group¹ *n. People were sitting in small groups.* clique, cluster, crowd, gang, set, team

group² *v. Group these objects according to weight.* arrange,

Growls, Grunts, and Other Animal Noises

Bees buzz
Cats meow
Cows moo
Dogs bark and growl
Ducks quack
Horses neigh
Lions roar
Mice squeak
Owls hoot
Pigs grunt
Roosters crow
Seals grunt
Snakes hiss
Wolves howl

categorize, classify, order, put in order, sort

grow *v. The hostages' fears are growing.* increase, multiply, spread *decline
These plants grow best in a shady spot. develop, flourish, germinate, shoot up, sprout

growl *v. The dog growled at us.* bay, snap, snarl

grown-up *adj. Our teacher has two grown-up children.* adult, fully grown, mature

growth *n. There has been a growth in numbers.* expansion, increase, proliferation, rise

grumble *v. He is always grumbling about how much he hates his job.* complain, moan, mutter, protest, whine (*informal*)

grumpy *adj. I'm always grumpy in the morning.* annoyed, bad-tempered, cross, crotchety, irritable, sour, touchy (*informal*) *cheerful

guarantee *n. The town council gave a guarantee that it would not sell the playing fields.* commitment, pledge, promise, warranty

guard[1] *n. Guards stood outside the entrance.* defender, sentry, warden

guard[2] *v. Policemen guard foreign embassies.* defend, patrol, protect, shield, watch over *attack

guess *v. If you don't know the answer, guess.* conjecture, estimate, judge, speculate, surmise

guest *n. We had several guests staying with us over the summer.* caller, visitor

guide[1] *n. A guide took us around the town.* conductor, escort, leader

guide[2] *v. Railroad staff guided the passengers to safety.* conduct, direct, escort, lead, shepherd, steer, usher

guilty *adj. He is guilty of the crime of murder.* at fault, blameworthy, culpable, responsible, to blame *innocent
I feel guilty because I told a lie. abashed, ashamed, remorseful, repentant, sorry

gush *v. Thousands of gallons of crude oil gushed into the sea after the oil tanker sunk.* flow, pour, run, spout, spurt, stream, surge

gust *n. There was a sudden gust of wind.* blast, blow, rush, squall

Hh

habit *n. I've gotten out of the habit of running every morning.* custom, practice, routine

Habitations

Apartment
Bungalow
Cabin
Castle
Chalet
Chateau
Cottage
Duplex
Estate
Hacienda
House
Hut
Igloo
Lodge
Mansion
Mobile home
Palace
Ranch
Shack
Shanty
Villa

haggle *v. They expect you to haggle over the price.* argue, bargain, barter, negotiate

hall *n. Please wait in the hall.* entrance, foyer, lobby, vestibule

hammer *v. Karim hammered on the door.* bang, beat, knock, pound

hand *v. Would you hand me my glasses, please?* deliver, give, pass, reach for

handle *v. Please handle the goods with care.* feel, finger, grasp, hold, manage, touch

handsome *adj. I met a very handsome man at the party.* attractive, good-looking, gorgeous, striking, hot (*informal*), hunky (*informal*) *****ugly**

handy *adj. A thesaurus is so handy when you're writing stories.* convenient, helpful, useful *****useless**

hang *v. Streamers hung from the telephone poles.* be suspended, dangle, droop, swing

happen *v. What's happening?*

occur, take place, come to pass (*literary*)

happiness *n. I wish you lots of happiness in the future.* bliss, contentment, delight, enjoyment, joy ***sadness**

happy *adj. She always seems so happy.* cheerful, content, contented, glad, jubilant, overjoyed, pleased ***sad**

hard *adj. This ground is too hard to dig.* firm, rigid, solid, stiff, stony ***soft**
I found the math homework very hard. complicated, demanding, difficult, tough ***easy**
He has a very hard heart. callous, hardhearted, pitiless, ruthless, severe, stern, tough ***gentle**

hardly *adv. I hardly recognized you.* barely, only just, scarcely
I hardly ever go to the movies these days. infrequently, rarely, seldom

harm[1] *n. Smoking during pregnancy can cause harm to the baby.* damage, injury, mischief, ruin

harm[2] *v. My brother wouldn't harm a fly.* abuse, hurt, injure, mistreat, lay a finger on (*informal*)

harmful *adj. This article talks about the harmful effects of smoking.* damaging, dangerous, ill, injurious, unhealthy ***harmless**

harmless *adj. Don't worry; it's harmless.* benign, gentle, innocuous, safe ***harmful**

harmony *n. Both classes worked together in harmony.* accord, agreement, cooperation, goodwill, unity

harsh *adj. She has a very harsh voice.* grating, jarring, rasping, raucous, rough ***soft**
He was a harsh military dictator. cruel, heartless, merciless, ruthless, severe, strict ***mild**

hassle *n. Waiting at the checkout is a real hassle.* annoyance, bother, difficulty, inconvenience, nuisance, struggle, pain (*informal*)

hasty *adj. I left after eating a hasty breakfast.* hurried, quick, rushed, speedy ***slow**

hate *v. I hate living in the country.* abhor, be unable to bear/stand, despise, detest, loathe ***love**

have *v. We used to have a much bigger car.* be the owner of, own, possess
I had trouble finding your house on the map. experience, undergo
What did you have for breakfast? consume, drink, eat

have to *v. I have to go home now; it's late.* be obliged to, must, ought, should

hazy *adj. I have only hazy memories of my childhood.* dim, indistinct, uncertain, unclear, vague ***clear**

heal *v. This cream will heal the cut.* cure, mend, soothe, treat

healthy *adj. I'm very lucky; I've got three healthy children.* fit, hearty, thriving, vigorous, well ***sick**

The school cafeteria serves a range of very healthy foods. beneficial, nourishing, nutritious, wholesome ***unhealthy**

heap *n. All of his clothes lay in a heap.* mass, mound, pile, stack

hear *v. I could hear someone whistling.* catch, detect, listen to, overhear

heat *n. The heat made me feel very tired.* high temperature, hot weather, warmth

heavy *adj. I've got a very heavy suitcase.* bulky, hefty, ponderous, weighty ***light**

hectic *adj. Life is very hectic for me at the moment.* busy, excited, fast, frantic, frenzied ***quiet**

height *n. What's the height of this building?* altitude, elevation, stature

He resigned, even though he was at the height of his career. peak, pinnacle, top, zenith

help¹ *n. We need more help in the kitchen.* aid, assistance, relief, support

help² *v. I helped Kelly carry her bags into the hotel.* aid, assist, give assistance to,

Headgear

Balaclava
Beret
Boater
Bonnet
Cap
Fedora
Fez
Glengarry

Hat
Helmet
Homburg
Hood
Kepi
Panama
Sombrero
Southwester

Stetson
Tam-o'-shanter
Top hat
Toque
Trilby
Turban
Tyrolean hat
Yarmulke

lend a hand ***hinder**

helpful *adj. The salesclerk was very helpful.* caring, considerate, kind, neighborly, obliging

A thesaurus is helpful when writing stories. beneficial, handy, practical, useful, worthwhile ***useless**

helping *n. Could I have a second helping of pie, please?* piece, portion, ration, serving

helpless *adj. The tiny kitten is completely helpless.* defenseless, dependent, incapable, powerless, vulnerable, weak

hesitate *v. He hesitated before answering.* falter, pause, wait, waver, hem and haw (*informal*)

hidden *adj. Hidden treasure was supposedly somewhere on the island.* concealed, covered, out of sight, unseen, veiled

hide *v. The dog hid the bone.* bury, conceal, cover, stash (*informal*) ***reveal**

high *adj. This town has lots of high buildings.* elevated, lofty, tall, towering ***low**
Jodie has a high voice. high-pitched, piercing, shrill, soprano ***low**

hill *n. The walkers finally reached the top of the hill.* rise, slope

hinder *v. Unfortunately, the bad weather hindered the rescue efforts.* frustrate, hamper, impede, obstruct,

thwart ***help**

hindrance *n. The onboard computer can sometimes be more of a hindrance than a help.* barrier, handicap, impediment, obstacle, obstruction ***help**

hint *v. Dominic hinted to his parents that he would like a new bike for Christmas.* give clues, indicate, insinuate, intimate, let it be known, suggest

hire *v. The company hired a plane to take its staff to the conference.* charter, lease, rent

hit[1] *n. The show was a huge hit.* sellout, success, triumph

hit[2] *v. The man hit his horse.* beat, punch, slap, spank, strike, whack (*informal*)
The truck hit the car at high speed. bump into, collide with, crash into, strike

hobby *n. My hobbies are football and baseball.* amusement, interest, leisure activity, pastime

hold *v. Could you hold my bag for a minute, please?* carry, clasp, grasp, grip, take
This briefcase holds all of my files. accommodate, comprise, contain, have room for

hole *n. There's a big hole in the roof.* gap, opening, slot

hollow *adj. The cylinder is hollow.* empty, vacant ***full**

holy *adj. This is a holy place.*

blessed, consecrated, hallowed, religious, sacred

honest *adj. Luckily my wallet was turned in by an honest man.* decent, honorable, law-abiding, principled, trustworthy, upright ***dishonest**

Please give me an honest answer. candid, frank, sincere, truthful

honesty *n. Honesty is the best policy.* integrity, morality, sincerity, truthfulness

Hues

A hue is a tint or variety of a color.

Blue: aquamarine, azure, indigo, sapphire, turquoise
Brown: amber, auburn, beige, chestnut, chocolate, dun, fawn, khaki
Green: apple, emerald, jade, moss, olive, pea, sea
Orange: carrot, tangerine
Purple: amethyst, heliotrope, lilac, magenta, mauve, violet
Red: cardinal, cerise, cherry, crimson, pink, salmon, scarlet, terra cotta
Yellow: apricot, canary, citron, lemon, saffron

hope *v. I hope to see you again.* anticipate, desire, expect, want

hopeful *adj. Doctors are hopeful that the president will be out of the hospital soon.* confident, expectant, optimistic, positive ***pessimistic**

hopeless *adj. It was a hopeless situation.* despairing, desperate, irremediable, very grave ***hopeful**

horrible *adj. What a horrible thing to happen to us!* atrocious, awful, dreadful, horrid, objectionable, shocking ***nice**

horror *n. People were screaming in horror when they saw the car accident.* dread, fear, fright, panic, shock ***pleasure**

hostile *adj. The Democrats launched a hostile attack on the Republicans.* aggressive, antagonistic, bitter, malevolent, unfriendly, vicious ***friendly**

hot *adj. It's very hot in here.* baking, boiling, roasting, sweltering, warm ***cold**
This chili is really hot. fiery, peppery, piquant, pungent, sharp, spicy, strong

house *n. This is the house where I grew up.* home, property, residence, abode (*formal*), dwelling (*formal*)

howl *v. I could hear the dog howling.* bay, cry, yelp

huddle *v. They all huddled together.* cluster, crowd, flock, gather, herd

hug *v. My mom hugged me.* clasp, cuddle, embrace

huge *adj. Blue whales are huge animals.* colossal, enormous, gigantic, immense, vast ***tiny**

hum *v. An insect was humming softly nearby.* buzz, drone, throb, whir

hungry *adj. I'm hungry; let's have something to eat.* famished, ravenous, starving ***full**

hunt *v. It is illegal to hunt deer in the park.* chase, pursue, stalk, track, trail

hurdle *n. Getting permission for an extension is the first hurdle we face.* barrier, difficulty, obstacle, obstruction, problem

hurry *v. Sorry, I must hurry to catch my train.* dash, go quickly, rush, speed up, burn rubber (*informal*), get a move on (*informal*), step on it (*informal*)

hurt[1] *v. I've hurt my foot.* harm, injure, wound
Your letter hurt me. distress, upset, wound ***cheer (up)**

hurt[2] *adj. I feel very hurt by your comments.* distressed, offended, sad, upset ***pleased**

hurtful *adj. Those were very hurtful remarks.* cruel, cutting, distressing, unkind, upsetting, wounding ***pleasant**

hut *n. They stayed in a hut in the mountains.* cabin, shack, shanty, shed, shelter

Ii

idea *n. I've got an idea; let's put up the tent.* plan, proposal, suggestion
I've got a vague idea of what my story will be about. concept, image, impression, notion, thought

ideal *adj. The weather was ideal for sailing.* excellent, model, perfect ***wrong**

identify *v. The police identified the thief from his fingerprints.* detect, distinguish, know, recognize, spot
I identified with the protagonist of the story. connect with, relate to, see eye to eye

idiot *n. Which idiot has hidden the key?* fool, imbecile, dimwit (*informal*), nitwit (*informal*)

idiotic *adj. That's the most idiotic idea I've ever heard.* crazy, foolish, silly, stupid, dumb (*informal*), harebrained (*informal*) ***sensible**

idle *adj. He's so idle; he sits watching television all day long.* indolent, lazy, shiftless, slothful ***busy**

ignorant *adj. Many teenagers are ignorant of the dangers of* *chatrooms.* misinformed, oblivious (to), unaware, uninformed, clueless (*informal*) *****aware

ignore *v. I said hello to Bethany, but she ignored me.* disregard, pass over, pay no attention to, snub, give the cold shoulder (*informal*)
You can ignore question two and go on to number three. disregard, neglect, omit, overlook, pay no attention to, skip

ill *adj. Zoe isn't here today; she's ill.* ailing, infirm, sick, unwell, out of sorts (*informal*), under the weather (*informal*) *****healthy
We studied the ill effects of tobacco. adverse, bad, damaging, evil, harmful *****good

illegal *adj. It's illegal to use a cell phone while driving.* against the law, criminal, illicit, unlawful *****legal

illness *n. He's suffering from a rare illness.* ailment, disease, disorder, sickness

imaginary *adj. Narnia is an imaginary land created by the writer C. S. Lewis.* fanciful, fictitious, make-believe, nonexistent, unreal *****real

imagination *n. Use your imagination.* creative powers, creativity, inventiveness, mental powers, vision

imagine *v. Imagine how those people must feel.* envisage, picture, think, visualize
I imagine you have come to apologize. assume, expect, presume, suppose

immediate *adj. It won't be possible to send an immediate reply.* instant, instantaneous, prompt

immediately *adv. Stop what you are doing immediately!* at once, directly, now, right away, without delay

impatient *adj. The people in the line were getting impatient.* agitated, edgy, intolerant, irritable, restless *****patient

important *adj. It's important to lock all of the windows before you go out.* critical, essential, imperative, necessary, vital *****optional
This is a very important matter. critical, serious, significant, substantial *****petty

impossible *adj. It's impossible to play tennis in this weather.* hopeless, impractical, not possible, out of the question *****possible

impress *v. He tried to impress me by talking about his new car.* affect, influence, inspire, sway

impression *n. I get the impression that you'd prefer to do something else.* belief, feeling, idea, suspicion

imprison v. *She was imprisoned for drug smuggling.* confine, incarcerate, jail, lock up, send to jail ***release**

improve v. *I went on the school exchange program to improve my French.* boost, make better, make progress with, refine, brush up (*informal*) ***spoil**

impulsive adj. *I'm too impulsive; I need to stop and think before I do anything.* hasty, impetuous, rash, reckless ***cautious**

inappropriate adj. *Shouting in a hospital is inappropriate behavior.* improper, incorrect, unfitting, unseemly, unsuitable, wrong ***appropriate**

inclined adj. *She's inclined to be a bit lazy.* disposed, liable, prone

include v. *This chapter includes a lot of information.* comprise, contain, cover, encompass, incorporate ***exclude**

income n. *Many families have a low income.* earnings, pay, revenue, salary, wages

incomplete adj. *The work was incomplete at the time of his death.* partial, undone, unfinished ***complete**

inconvenient adj. *Being without my car is very inconvenient.* annoying, awkward, difficult, troublesome ***convenient**

increase[1] n. *There's been an increase in demand for ice cream this summer.* boost, growth, rise, surge ***decrease**

increase[2] v. *I'm determined to increase my scores this year.* add to, boost, enhance, heighten, improve, raise ***decrease**

incredible adj. *She did an incredible job on her test.* amazing, fantastic, terrific, wonderful
It's such an incredible story that I'm not sure if I believe it. far-fetched, implausible, unbelievable

independent adj. *Montenegro is now an independent country.* autonomous, free, self-governing, self-reliant, separate

indicate v. *The big yellow arrow indicates the route.* denote, point out, show

individual adj. *We will examine every individual complaint.* separate, single

inefficient adj. *I'm very inefficient at fixing things.* incapable, incompetent, ineffective, unskilled, hopeless (*informal*), useless (*informal*) ***efficient**

inexperienced adj. *He's still an inexperienced actor.* green, immature, raw, unqualified, untrained, callow (*literary*) ***experienced**

infectious adj. *Colds are infectious.* communicable, contagious

influence[1] n. *The Beatles had a*

lasting influence on British pop music. effect, force, impact, sway

influence² *v. In what ways did your father influence you?* affect, have an effect on, impress, inspire

inform *v. Please inform us of any change of address.* advise, let know, notify, tell, warn

informal *adj. The party was an informal affair.* casual, easygoing, relaxed, simple *formal

information *n. Do you have any information about our new neighbors?* data, details, intelligence, knowledge, news

injure *v. He injured his foot playing soccer.* damage, harm, hurt, wound

innocent *adj. He didn't steal the money; he's completely innocent.* blameless, faultless, guiltless, not guilty, in the clear (*informal*) *guilty
Stephanie was really innocent before she moved to the big city. artless, gullible, inexperienced, ingenuous, naive, trusting, unsophisticated, unworldly *corrupt

inquire *v. I'd like to inquire about times of trains to New York.* ask, ask a question, ask for information, check, look into

inside *adj. Please put your mittens in your inside coat pocket.* indoor, inner, interior, internal

insist *v. I insist that you come with me to see the principal.* demand, request, require
She insisted on keeping the news a secret. assert, emphasize, maintain, promise, swear

inspect *v. It is Raj's job to inspect the finished products.* assess, check, examine, monitor, oversee

instance *n. In this instance I agree with you.* case, example, occasion, occurrence

instant¹ *n. Beware! The weather up here in the mountains can change in an instant.* flash, minute, moment, blink of an eye (*informal*), jiffy (*informal*)

instant² *adj. This bank account gives account holders instant access to all of their money.* immediate, instantaneous, on the spot, rapid

instantly *adv. I e-mailed Jack, and he replied instantly.* at once, immediately, promptly, right away

instead *adv. The train drivers were on strike today, so I took the bus instead.* alternatively, as an alternative

instead of *prep. I can come instead of my sister if you prefer.* in place of, rather than

instructions *n. pl. Please make*

Instruments

Accordion	Fiddle	Organ
Bagpipes	Fife	Piano
Balalaika	Flute	Piccolo
Banjo	French horn	Recorder
Bassoon	Glockenspiel	Saxophone
Bells	Guitar	Synthesizer
Bugle	Harmonica	Tambourine
Castanets	Harp	Triangle
Cello	Harpsichord	Trombone
Clarinet	Hurdy-gurdy	Trumpet
Cornet	Kazoo	Tuba
Cymbals	Kettledrum	Ukulele
Didjeridoo	Lute	Viola
Double bass	Lyre	Violin
Drum	Mandolin	Whistle
Dulcimer	Maraca	Xylophone
Electric guitar	Oboe	Zither

sure to read the instructions carefully. directions, guidelines, rubric (*formal*)

insult *v. I know that people insult me behind my back.* make rude comments about, offend, slander, snub ***flatter**

intend *v. I intend to spend the weekend catching up on housework.* aim, be determined, plan, propose

intense *adj. The heat at noon was intense.* extreme, great, strong ***mild**

intention *n. My intention is to go to college and study medicine.*

aim, goal, intent, objective, plan

interesting *adj. I find history a very interesting subject.* absorbing, appealing, entertaining, fascinating
*boring

interfere *v. I really wouldn't want to interfere in his private life; it's his business.* intrude, meddle, pry into, poke one's nose into (*informal*)

interrupt *v. Excuse me, but may I interrupt for a minute?* break in, interject, intrude, butt in (*informal*)

introduce *v. May I introduce you to our new secretary?* acquaint with, present
The principal has introduced some new rules. bring in, launch, propose

introduction *n. The book has a really good introduction.* foreword, preface, prelude, prologue

invade *v. The Roman army invaded Great Britain in A.D. 43.* attack, occupy, seize, storm
*defend

invent *v. Some people say it wasn't Alexander Graham Bell who invented the telephone.* conceive, create, develop, devise, originate, think up

invention *n. The computer is a wonderful invention.* contrivance, creation, design, discovery, gadget

investigate *v. Police are investigating the bank robbery.* examine, look into, make inquiries about, research, study

invisible *adj. The scientist had a cloak that made him invisible.* concealed, hidden, out of sight, unable to be seen, unseen
*visible

invite *v. I'm inviting the whole class to my birthday party.* ask, request the presence of, summon

involve *v. The concert always involves so much preparation.* demand, entail, necessitate, need, require

involved *adj. He got very involved with his community-service project.* attached to, committed to, invested in
The setup of the robot was quite involved. complex, complicated, difficult

issue *n. The first issue of the magazine will go on sale next week.* copy, edition, impression, installment
At this school, bullying is an issue that we take very seriously. affair, matter, problem, question, subject, topic

itch *v. This wool sweater makes me itch all over.* prickle, scratch, tingle

item *n. Click on an item to add it to your shopping basket.* article, object, product, thing

Jj

jail *n. The murderer was sent to jail.* penitentiary, prison

jam¹ *n. (informal) We got ourselves into a jam.* dilemma, predicament, quandary, tricky situation, fix *(informal)*, pickle *(informal)*

jam² *v. The door has jammed.* become wedged, get stuck, stick
The passengers all jammed into one train. crowd, crush, pack, squeeze

jar *n. He gave her a jar of jam.* container, pot

jealous *adj. Cinderella's ugly stepsisters were jealous of her beauty.* begrudging, envious, resentful, green with envy *(informal)*

jealousy *n. Jealousy is an unpleasant emotion.* envy, resentment, spite

jeer *v. The fans jeered at the opposing team.* boo, deride, insult, laugh at, mock, ridicule, taunt ***praise**

jerk *v. She jerked back her head.* pull, tug, wrench, yank

jet *n. The dentist uses a machine that squirts a jet of water.* spray, spurt, squirt, stream

jewel *n. Ali Baba saw the thieves hide the jewels.* gem, gemstone,

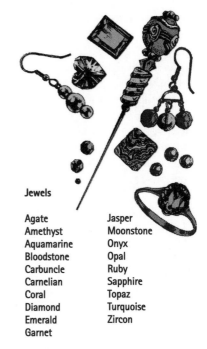

Jewels

Agate	Jasper
Amethyst	Moonstone
Aquamarine	Onyx
Bloodstone	Opal
Carbuncle	Ruby
Carnelian	Sapphire
Coral	Topaz
Diamond	Turquoise
Emerald	Zircon
Garnet	

precious stone

jingle *v. The money in his pocket jingled as he walked.* clink, jangle, ring, tinkle

job *n. A tailor's job is making and fixing clothes.* career, employment, line of business, livelihood, living, occupation, profession, trade
Yasmin is looking for a new job. position, post, situation
Mom gave each of us a job to do. assignment, chore, errand, project, task

join *v. Join these two cables together.* attach, combine, connect, link, unite ***separate**

Danny intends to join the army as soon as he leaves school. enlist in, enroll in, enter, sign up for *****leave

joint *adj. We've got a joint bank account.* combined, common, mutual, shared, united *****individual

joke *n. I'm afraid I don't know many jokes.* anecdote, prank, pun, wisecrack, gag (*informal*)

journey *n. The journey took three hours.* excursion, trip, voyage

judge *n. The DJ was asked to be a judge for the latest TV talent contest.* adjudicator, official, referee, umpire

jug *n. A jug of ice-cold water had been placed on each table.* carafe, flask, jar, pitcher, ewer (*literary*)

jumble *n. Ellie was sorting out a jumble of old toys, clothes, and magazines.* heap, hodgepodge, medley, mess, mixture, pile, tangle

jump *v. He jumped down from the wall.* bound, leap, spring

junction *n. After around two miles you'll come to a junction in the road; take the road on the left.* crossroad, intersection

junk *n.* (*informal*) *Our garage is full of junk.* clutter, debris, garbage, trash

just¹ *adj. A just law handled the criminals.* evenhanded, fair, honest, impartial, sound, unbiased *****unfair

just² *adv. That cup of coffee was just what I wanted.* exactly, in every respect, in every way, precisely
He has just arrived at the airport. a moment ago, a short time ago, very recently
There are just a few cakes left. merely, no more than, only, simply

justice *n. Justice must prevail.* equality, evenhandedness, fairness, fair play, honesty, impartiality

jut *v. The balcony juts out over the street.* extend, overhang, project, stick out

Kk

keep *v. The policewoman allowed me to keep the money I found in the street.* hold, retain, retain possession of, hang on to (*informal*) *****give up
Come on, keep going! Don't stop now! carry on, continue, go on, persevere, persist *****give up

key¹ *n. The key to what the symbols mean can be found at the bottom of the map.* answer, clue, explanation, guide, solution

key² *adj. Include only the key points of the report.* basic, crucial, essential, fundamental, main, major, most important, vital

kick *v. He kicked the ball down the field toward the opponents'*

goal. boot, hit, punt, strike with the foot

kidnap *v. The gang kidnapped the banker's son and demanded a ransom.* abduct, capture,

"A Little Knowledge Is a Dangerous Thing" and Other Misquotes

Many of the familiar quotations that we use from literature, history, or the world of entertainment are incorrect adaptations of the originals. Greta Garbo did not say, "I want to be alone." Her true words were "I like to be alone." Shakespeare did not say, "Discretion is the better part of valor." The correct quotation is "The better part of valor is discretion." Here are some more, with the correct original versions printed in italic type:

From Shakespeare:
Alas, poor Yorick: I knew him well.
Alas, poor Yorick; I knew him,
Horatio: a fellow of infinite jest
(*Hamlet*)

O Romeo, Romeo! wherefore art thou, Romeo?
O Romeo, Romeo! wherefore art thou Romeo?
(*Romeo and Juliet*)
(Note the incorrect presence of the second comma. "Wherefore" means "why," not "where.")

All that glitters is not gold . . .
All that glisters is not gold . . .
(*The Merchant of Venice*)

From the King James Bible:
Pride goes before a fall . . .
Pride goeth before destruction and an haughty spirit
before a fall . . .
(Proverbs)

Money is the root of all evil . . .
For the love of money is the root of all evil . . .
(Timothy)

To go the way of all flesh . . .
And, behold, this day I am going the way of all
the earth . . .
(Joshua)

Other sources:
Water, water, everywhere, and not a drop to drink . . .
Water, water, everywhere, nor any drop to drink . . .
("The Rime of the Ancient Mariner")

A little knowledge is a dangerous thing . . .
A little learning is a dang'rous thing . . .
(Alexander Pope)

Play it again, Sam.
(Humphrey Bogart in the movie *Casablanca*)
Play it, Sam. Play "As Time Goes By."
(Ingrid Bergman in the movie *Casablanca*)

hijack, seize, snatch

kill *v. He was sentenced to at least 200 years in prison for killing dozens of people.* assassinate, massacre, murder, put to death, slaughter, slay

kind[1] *n. The market sells all kinds of things.* category, sort, style, type, variety

kind[2] *adj. The kind lady gave us candy.* benevolent, bighearted, caring, considerate, good-natured, kindly, thoughtful ***unkind**

kindness *n. Thanks for your kindness.* benevolence, consideration, generosity, kindliness, tenderness, thoughtfulness

king *n. There have been six kings of England named George.* head of state, monarch, ruler, sovereign

kneel *v. After the hymn, the congregation knelt and prayed.* bend down, bow down, genuflect

knock *v. I knocked on the door.* bang, hammer, hit, rap, strike, tap

knock down *v. The workers knocked down the apartment building in just three days.* demolish, destroy, flatten, level, raze to the ground ***build**

knock out *v. The boxer was knocked out in the first round of the match.* daze, level, render

unconscious, stun, deck (*informal*)

know *v. I didn't know anyone at the party, so I went home.* be acquainted with, be familiar with, recognize
I'm afraid I don't know the answers to any of your questions at the moment. be aware of, be informed about, have knowledge of, realize

knowledge *n. Taxi drivers need to have a thorough knowledge of the layout of the town.* acquaintance (with), awareness, command, familiarity (with), grasp, understanding

Ll

label *n. The price is on the label.* slip, sticker, tab, tag, ticket

lack[1] *n. Because of the lack of rain, the reservoirs are almost empty.* absence, dearth, deficiency, insufficiency, scarcity, shortage

lack[2] *v. More than one billion people in the world lack clean drinking water.* be deficient in, be short of, have need of, need, require ***have**

land[1] *n. The farm has a lot of land.* grounds, terrain, territory
He has visited many lands. area, country, nation, place, state

land[2] *v. The plane landed safely.*

arrive, touch down

lap¹ *n. I did four laps of the racetrack.* circle, circuit, loop
The kitten sat on her lap. knees, thighs

lap² *v. The cat lapped milk from the bowl.* drink, lick up, sip

large *adj. Our gym isn't very large.* big, huge, sizable, spacious, substantial *small
I needed to drink a large amount of water after the race.
abundant, ample, copious, great, plentiful, profuse *small

last¹ *v. The movie lasts for around two hours.* continue, endure, go on, persist, take

last² *adj. I'm on the last page now.* closing, concluding, end, final, latter, ultimate *first
I was on vacation last week.
former, most recent, past, preceding, previous *next

late *adj. You're late; the class has already started.* belated, delayed, overdue, tardy *early

lately *adv. There have been a lot of good movies lately.* in the past month/week, of late, recently

laugh *v. The children laughed quietly.* chortle, chuckle, giggle, snicker, titter
The crowd was laughing out loud at the comedy show.
cackle, guffaw, be in stitches (*informal*), be rolling in the aisles (*informal*), fall over (*informal*)

laugh at *v. My friends laughed at me when I fell over.* deride, jeer at, make fun of, mock, ridicule, taunt, tease

law *n. The government has passed several new laws this year.* act, edict, regulation, rule, ruling

lay *v. Alfie laid his coat on the ground.* deposit, place, put, set, spread

layer *n. There was a layer of snow on the ground.* blanket, coat, coating, covering, sheet

lazy *adj. He's so lazy that he can't even be bothered to fry an egg.* idle, inactive, indolent, shiftless, slothful, sluggish

lead *v. The senator led the delegation.* be in charge of, direct, head, preside over
The teacher led us into the cave.
conduct, direct, escort, guide, shepherd, steer, usher *follow

leader *n. Naz was chosen to be the group leader.* boss, captain, chief, commander, guide, head

leak *v. Gas leaked from the pipe.* escape, exude, flow out, ooze, seep, trickle

lean *v. The portrait painter asked the model to lean her head forward.* bend, curve, incline, slant, slope, tilt

leap *v. Look before you leap.* bound, jump, spring

learn *v. I'd like to learn another foreign language.* gain

knowledge of, master, memorize, study, pick up (*informal*)
Stuart has just learned that he didn't get the job. become aware, be informed, discover, find out, hear

least *adj. The team with the least number of points at the end of the year will be removed from the league.* fewest, lowest, slightest, smallest ***most**

leave *v. The train leaves in five minutes.* depart, go, set off ***arrive**
He made her a promise that he would never leave her. abandon, desert, quit, turn one's back on, forsake (*literary*)

leave out *v. Leave out any question that you don't understand.* disregard, exclude, ignore, miss out, omit, pass over, skip ***include**

legal *adj. I'll only do it if it's legal.* allowed, authorized, lawful, legitimate, permitted, within the law ***illegal**

legend *n. A book of legends was on display at the library.* fable, myth, story, tale

legendary *adj. The stories about the Loch Ness monster are legendary.* fictitious, mythical

lend *v. Can you please lend me some money?* advance, loan, provide with, supply with ***borrow**

lengthen *v. Please lengthen the line on the paper.* extend, prolong, stretch

less *adj. I get much less allowance money than my sister.* a smaller amount of, not so much ***more**

let *v. My parents won't let me go to the dance.* allow, authorize, grant permission to, permit ***forbid**

let down *v. He let down his teammates.* abandon, betray, disappoint, leave in the lurch (*informal*)

let off *v. The principal let him off.* absolve, forgive, pardon, reprieve ***punish**

level[1] *n. You've advanced to the next level.* grade, stage, standard

level[2] *adj. The kitchen floor isn't level.* even, flat, horizontal, smooth ***uneven**

liar *n. You can't trust her; she's a liar.* cheat, deceiver, fibber, perjurer, teller of tales

lie[1] *n. No one believed his lies.* falsehood, fib, untruth, whopper (*informal*)

lie[2] *v. I will lie on the sofa all afternoon.* loll, lounge, recline, relax, sprawl, stretch out
You lied to me. fib, make things up

lift *v. I can't lift this box; it's too heavy.* elevate, hoist, hold up, raise

light[1] *n. I could see the light of the candle.* brightness, glare, glow,

Lights

Arc lamp
Candle
Chandelier
Desk lamp
Electric light
Flashlight
Fluorescent light
Footlights
Gaslight
Headlight
Lantern
Night-light
Reading light
Spotlight
Sunlamp
Table lamp
Torch

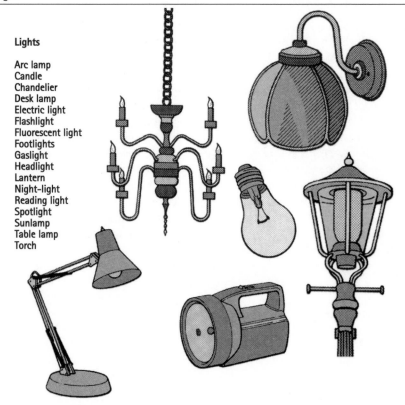

illumination, radiance
light² *v. The Boy Scouts lit a fire.*
ignite, kindle, put a match to, start
light³ *adj. I prefer light colors.* faint,
pale, pastel ***dark**
Luckily my suitcase is quite light.
lightweight, portable ***heavy**
like¹ *v. I like all of the teachers at
this school.* admire, approve of,
be fond of, look up to, love
***dislike**
like² *prep. You look just like my
mother when she was a little girl.*
akin to, identical to, similar to,
the same as
likely *adj. The most likely result
is a change in leadership.*
anticipated, expected, possible,
probable, in the cards
(*informal*) ***unlikely**
limit¹ *n. There's a limit to the
number of visitors allowed per
patient.* ceiling, cutoff point,
maximum, restriction
limit² *v. My parents have limited
the number of people I can
invite.* cap, confine, ration,
restrain, restrict

line n. *He drew a line.* dash, streak, strip, stripe
Form a line outside the door. file, procession, queue, row

linger v. *Some people lingered in the lobby after the show.* dally, dawdle, delay, loiter, remain, stay, stay behind, wait

link[1] n. *What's the link between these three objects?* bond, common factor, connection, relationship

link[2] v. *The websites are linked to an online supermarket.* associate, connect, join, unite *separate

list n. *Here is a list of everyone going on the trip.* record, register, roster, schedule, table

listen v. *Listen carefully.* hear, lend an ear, pay attention, be all ears (*informal*), hark (*literary*), hearken (*literary*)

litter n. *Please throw out your litter.* garbage, refuse, trash, waste

little adj. *We live in a little cottage.* minuscule, minute, small, tiny *large
I've got very little time to myself these days. hardly any, limited, not much *much

live[1] (*rhymes with* give) v. *He lived until he was well into his 90s.* be alive, breathe, exist, survive

live[2] (*rhymes with* hive) adj. *I don't like it when medical experiments are carried out on live animals.* alive, breathing, living *dead

lively adj. *A roomful of lively toddlers brightens my day.* active, animated, boisterous, energetic, exuberant, frisky *sleepy
Downtown is always very lively on Friday nights. bustling, busy, buzzing, vibrant *quiet

load[1] n. *The truck was carrying a heavy load.* burden, cargo, consignment, freight

load[2] v. *They loaded up the van with their equipment.* fill, fill up, pack, stack

loan n. *The bank agreed to give me a loan.* advance, credit, overdraft

local adj. *I support my local government.* district, municipal, provincial, regional

lock[1] n. *The lock is jammed.* bolt, catch, fastener, latch

lock[2] v. *Lock the door when you leave.* bolt, fasten, secure

loiter v. *A group of young men were loitering outside the store.* linger, lurk, skulk, hang around (*informal*)
Please don't loiter in the corridors between lessons. dally, dawdle, delay, dilly-dally (*informal*) *hurry

lone adj. *A lone piper played the bagpipes.* single, sole, solitary, solo, unaccompanied

lonely adj. *Maggie has been so

lonely since the death of her husband. alone, friendless, isolated, lonesome, forlorn (*literary*), forsaken (*literary*)

long¹ *v. I long for a good night's sleep.* crave, desire, hanker (after/for), look forward to, pine for, yearn for

long² *adj. All of the books in the His Dark Materials series are quite long.* expanded, extended, lengthy, drawn-out (*informal*) ***short**

look¹ *n. The company website has been given a new, more up-to-date look.* air, appearance, aspect

look² *v. I looked at the people around me.* gaze at, observe, stare at, study, view, watch
Mei-Ann looked quickly over her shoulder. glance, glimpse, peek, peep
The man looked angry. appear, seem

look for *v. I'm looking for my glasses; have you seen them?* hunt for, search for, seek, try to find ***find**

look like *v. I think that Duncan looks like his father did at that age.* be similar to, be the image of, resemble, take after

loose *adj. These pants are a little loose.* baggy, big, roomy, slack ***tight**
The dogs are loose. at large, at liberty, free, on the loose

lose *v. I've lost my new cell phone!* mislay, misplace ***find**
The Celtics have lost every game this season. be beaten, be defeated, suffer defeat ***win**

lost *adj. Two children are lost in the woods.* absent, gone, missing, vanished

lot *n. Our daughter, Susie, has a lot of friends.* a great deal, a large number, lots, many, plenty, loads (*informal*), tons (*informal*) ***few**

loud *adj. That radio is so loud that it has given me a headache.* blaring, deafening, earsplitting, noisy ***quiet**
Mr. Davies is wearing a very loud tie today. brash, flashy, garish, gaudy, tasteless, vulgar ***plain**

love¹ *n. Love is certainly a powerful, sometimes dangerous emotion.* adoration, affection, ardor, devotion, fondness, passion ***hate**

love² *v. Everyone knows that she loves all of her children.* adore, be devoted to, be fond of, cherish, dote on, feel great affection for, idolize, treasure, worship ***hate**

lovely *adj. They live in a lovely village set in the middle of a beautiful countryside.* beautiful, charming, delightful, picturesque, pleasant, pretty, quaint, scenic ***ugly**

Jed is a lovely man. adorable, agreeable, charming, pleasant, sweet ***nasty**

low *adj. There was a low wall running around the yard.* low-lying, short, small, squat ***high**
It was difficult to hear her speak because she had such a low voice. faint, inaudible, muffled, quiet, quietly spoken, soft ***loud**

luck *n. It was only by pure luck that I happened to find the letter.* chance, coincidence, destiny, fate, fortune, fluke (*informal*)

lucky *adj. I'm lucky to be able to eat practically anything I want without putting on weight.* blessed, charmed, favored, fortunate ***unlucky**

luggage *n. Some passengers have so much luggage that they will have to pay an excess fee.* baggage, belongings, suitcases, personal effects (*formal*)

lump *n. There is a large and painful lump growing on my forehead.* bulge, bump, protuberance, swelling
He bought a huge lump of his favorite cheese. bit, block, chunk, hunk, piece, slab, wedge

lurk *v. There was a strange man, dressed all in black, lurking in the bushes.* hide, lie in wait, loiter, prowl, skulk, slink

luxury *n. It's pleasant to enjoy a little luxury now and then.* affluence, comfort, opulence, richness, splendor, wealth
Life's little luxuries are what make it worth living. extra, extravagance, frill, indulgence, treat

Mm

machine *n. The work is normally done by a machine, not by a person.* appliance, engine, mechanical device

mad *adj. Dad was mad at me for scratching the car.* angry, fuming, furious, incensed, livid (*informal*) ***calm**

magazine *n. The store stocks a wide range of magazines.* journal, periodical, publication, glossy (*informal*)

magic *n. Harry Potter studied magic at Hogwarts.* sorcery, witchcraft, wizardry

magical *adj. This plant has magical powers.* extraordinary, magic, mysterious, occult, supernatural ***ordinary**

magician *n. The magician at Kieran's party made a bunch of flowers appear inside a balloon.* conjurer, illusionist, sorcerer, wizard

main *adj. We live just off a main street.* important, leading, major, primary, principal

mainly *adv. Crocodiles eat mainly fish.* chiefly, for the most part, generally, mostly, on the whole, predominantly, usually ***seldom**

major *adj. Drugs are a major problem in this neighborhood.* considerable, important, main, significant ***minor**

make *v. Let's make a tree house.* assemble, build, construct, fabricate, fashion, manufacture, produce ***destroy**
The thieves made the bank manager open the safe by threatening him. coerce, compel, drive, force, oblige
They made him the captain of the basketball team. appoint, designate, name, nominate

make up *v. That's not true; you made it up!* concoct, dream up, fabricate, invent
Sarah and Jessica made up after their argument. reconcile, bury the hatchet (*informal*), forgive and forget (*informal*), settle one's differences (*informal*)

man *n. That man is my father.* boy, male, fellow (*informal*), guy (*informal*)

manage *v. He manages the accounts department.* administer, be in charge of, control, direct, head, lead, run
You can go home if you want; I'll be able to manage alone. cope, fare, get along, get by ***struggle**

manager *n. The manager of the shoe department gave me a coupon.* boss, director, head, overseer, superintendent, supervisor

many *adj. There are many different types of spiders.* a great deal of, a large number of, a lot of, an abundance of, a plethora of, countless, lots of, numerous ***few**

map *n. The map shows where the treasure is hidden.* chart, diagram, plan, table

mark¹ *n. There are dirty marks on my shirt.* blotch, fleck, spot, stain, streak
Yellow marks on the curb mean that parking is prohibited. dot, sign, stripe, symbol
I got a good mark on my test. grade, score

mark² *v. The teacher spent her lunch hour marking homework.* assess, check, correct, evaluate

mask *v. Air fresheners mask the smell of stale food.* camouflage, conceal, cover up, disguise, hide ***reveal**

mass *adj. Protesters staged a mass demonstration against the planned invasion.* extensive, large, large-scale, widespread ***small**

match *v. These socks don't match.* be a pair, be the same, correspond, equal ***vary**

material *n. Julie's dress was made of silky material.* cloth, fabric, textile
If you need more material for your research, use the Internet. data, information, resources

meal *n. Breakfast is my favorite meal*

of the day. banquet, feast, snack

mean¹ *v What does this word mean?* denote, describe, express, represent, signify
I didn't mean to hurt him. aim, expect, intend, plan, set out

mean² *adj. Ken's so mean; he didn't even buy his mom a birthday card.* cold, cruel, hardhearted, low, vicious

meaning *n. If you don't know the meaning of a word, look it up in a dictionary.* definition, explanation, sense

measure *v. To measure the length of the line, you need a ruler.* calculate, determine, evaluate, gauge

meddle *v. Robin is always meddling in other people's private business.* interfere, intervene, intrude, pry, butt in (*informal*), poke one's nose in (*informal*)

medium *adj. In the United States, a BMW is thought of as a medium-size car.* average, normal, ordinary, standard

meet *v. I am supposed to meet my new neighbors after school.* become acquainted with, be introduced to

Measurements

Millimeter
Centimeter
Meter
Kilometer
Milliliter
Liter
Milligram
Gram
Kilogram
Ton

Inch
Foot
Yard
Mile
Cup
Pint
Quart
Gallon
Ounce
Pound
Ton

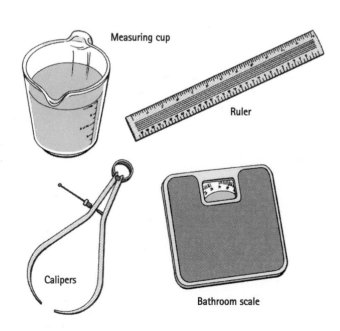

Measuring cup

Ruler

Calipers

Bathroom scale

The chess club meets in the library every Friday. assemble, congregate, convene, gather, get together

meeting n. Do you think you will be going to the meeting tomorrow? assembly, conference, gathering, workshop

melody n. I could listen to this melody forever. jingle, song, tune

melt v. The ice has already started to melt. defrost, dissolve, liquefy, soften, thaw *set

menace n. That boy is a real menace to the local community. danger, nuisance, risk, torment

mention v. I forgot to mention that there's a pottery class this evening. announce, declare, disclose, remark, reveal, say
Don't mention politics when you're talking to Sally. allude to, broach the subject of, refer to, speak about

mercy n. The prisoner begged for mercy. clemency, compassion, forgiveness, pity, forbearance (formal)

merge v. The roads merge in a few miles. amalgamate, blend, combine, converge, fuse, join, unite *separate

merit¹ n. I was awarded a certificate of merit by the principal. caliber, excellence, quality, talent, worth

merit² v. This work does not merit anything higher than a C grade. be worthy of, deserve, justify, warrant

mess n. Which one of you made all this mess in here? chaos, clutter, confusion, disorder, jumble *order

message n. Did you get my message yesterday about going to the movies? communication, missive, note

messy adj. Don't go to the interview looking messy. bedraggled, disheveled, slovenly, unkempt, scruffy (informal)
The room is very messy. cluttered, disorganized,

Metals

Aluminum
Brass
Bronze
Chromium
Copper
Gold
Iron
Lead
Manganese
Mercury
Nickel
Platinum
Silver
Steel
Tin
Zinc

Silver trophy

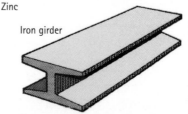

Iron girder

in disarray

method *n. Frying is a much quicker method of cooking than roasting.* manner, means, mode, procedure, system, technique, way

middle *n. They pitched their tent right in the middle of the forest.* center, core, heart, hub *****edge**

mild *adj. He is well known by everyone for his charm and mild manner.* calm, docile, easygoing, genial, gentle, meek, moderate *****harsh**

mind[1] *n. I said the very first thing that came into my mind.* brain, head, imagination, intellect, thoughts

mind[2] *v. Do you mind if I open the window?* be bothered, care, object
My granny minds us during the school holidays. care for, look after, take care of, tend *****neglect**
Mind you don't hurt yourself. be careful, beware, watch out

minister *n. We have a new minister at church.* clergyman, pastor, priest, rabbi

minor *adj. There are only a few minor problems to be taken care of.* lesser, slight, smaller, trifling, trivial, unimportant *****major**

miracle *n. It's an absolute miracle that you weren't injured.* marvel, phenomenon, supernatural event, wonder

mischief *n. My little brother is always up to mischief.* bad behavior, impishness, naughtiness, pranks

mischievous *adj. Mischievous little puppies, stop chewing my shoes!* badly behaved, destructive, impish, naughty

miser *n. The old miser never spends a penny.* cheapskate (*informal*), penny pincher (*informal*), Scrooge (*informal*), skinflint (*informal*), tightwad (*informal*)

miserable *adj. I had a bad flu and felt really miserable for days.* desolate, glum, sad, terrible, unhappy, down in the dumps (*informal*), forlorn (*literary*) *****cheerful**

misery *n. The television reporter described situations of appalling misery at the scene of the earthquake.* anguish, distress, grief, sorrow, suffering, unhappiness, woe *****happiness**

miss *v. The shot missed the target.* fail to hit, fall short of *****hit**
I really miss my old friends. lament the loss of, long to see, pine for, yearn for

mist *n. As it got warmer, the morning mist disappeared.* clouds, drizzle, fog, haze, moisture, vapor

mistake *n. I'm really sorry; I have made a terrible mistake.* blunder, error, fault, lapse, oversight, slip

mistreat v. *He was prosecuted for mistreating his pets.* abuse, harm, hurt, injure, maltreat (*formal*) ***care for**

mix v. *You need to mix the flour, sugar, and eggs together.* blend, combine, mingle, stir, whip ***separate**

mixture n. *The box contains a mixture of milk and dark chocolates.* assortment, blend, combination, medley, variety

mix up v. *Sometimes I mix up all my words.* confuse, jumble, muddle

moan v. *He lay on the bed, moaning in pain.* cry, groan, sigh, wail, whimper
Rachel can always find something to moan about. complain, grouch, grumble, whine (*informal*)

mob n. *The angry mob ran down the street.* crowd, gang, horde, throng

model[1] n. *The store sells a wide range of models of cars, aircraft, trains, and boats.* copy, replica, representation
I don't want an old washing machine; I want the latest model. brand, design, kind, sort, type, version

model[2] v. *She models good manners for her younger sister.* display, put on, represent, show

modern adj. *I prefer modern furniture to antique furniture.* contemporary, fashionable, new, state-of-the-art, the latest, up-to-date, hip (*informal*), trendy (*informal*) ***old-fashioned**

modest adj. *Sandy is very modest about her acting skills.* diffident, humble, unassuming ***vain**
Their house is very modest. plain, simple, unassuming

moist adj. *You need to apply the cream while your skin is still moist.* damp, dewy, humid ***dry**

moldy adj. *This cheese is moldy.* mildewy, musty, putrid, rotten ***fresh**

moment n. *I'll be with you in a moment.* instant, no time, second, jiffy (*informal*), the blink of an eye (*informal*)

money n. *Most people seem to think he married her for her money.* cash, prosperity, riches, wealth, bucks (*informal*), dough (*informal*), moola (*informal*)

mood n. *Paul is in a very bad mood today.* disposition, frame of mind, humor, state of mind, temper

moody adj. *Mrs. Ponting is so moody at times.* fickle, morose, sulky, sullen, temperamental ***cheerful**

more adj. *I'm going to need a little more time to finish the book.* additional, extra, further, supplementary ***less**

Money Around the World

afghani *Afghanistan*
balboa *Panama*
bolivar *Venezuela*
cedi *Ghana*
colon *Costa Rica, El Salvador*
dinar *Algeria, Bahrain, Iraq, Jordan, Kuwait, and more*
dollar *Australia, Bahamas, Canada, U.S., and more*
euro *European countries in the Eurozone*
forint *Hungary*
guarani *Paraguay*
kip *Laos*
krona *Iceland, Sweden*
krone *Denmark, Norway*
lek *Albania*
leu *Moldova, Romania*

lev *Bulgaria*
lira *Malta, Turkey*
naira *Nigeria*
peso *Argentina, Chile, Mexico, and more*
pound *United Kingdom and more*
rand *South Africa*
real *Brazil*
rial *Iran, Oman, Yemen*
ruble *Russia*
rupee *India, Pakistan, and more*
sol *Peru*
yen *Japan, Taiwan*
yuan *China*
zloty *Poland*

most *adv. Most of the people who were invited have arrived.* almost all, nearly all, the majority of

mostly *adv. We play tennis mostly in the summer and football mostly in the winter.* as a rule, generally, mainly, normally, principally, usually ***seldom**

motivate *v. I can't motivate myself to clean my room today.* impel, inspire, persuade, rouse, spark

motive *n. The police officers could find no motive for the crime.* basis, cause, grounds, purpose, reason

move *v. Would you help me move the table, please?* budge, carry, shift, transport

moving adj. *The story was very moving.* emotional, poignant, stirring, touching, affecting (*formal*)

much[1] adj. *They haven't got much money.* a great deal of, a lot of, an abundance of, lots of, plenty of *little

much[2] adv. *Leon hadn't changed much in ten years.* a lot, considerably, greatly, to a great extent *little

mumble v. *He mumbled something under his breath.* murmur, mutter, whisper *shout

must v. *I really must get going now, or I will miss my train.* be obliged to, have got to, have to, need to, ought to, should

mysterious adj. *Police are investigating the mysterious death of a former spy.* inexplicable, odd, puzzling, strange, unexplained

mystery n. *The mystery of the missing diver will never be solved.* enigma, problem, puzzle, riddle, secret

myth n. *Which is your favorite Greek myth?* epic, fable, legend

Nn

nag v. *My mom nagged me to clean my bedroom.* annoy, badger, pester, scold, hassle (*informal*)

naked adj. *The toddlers were playing naked in the pool.* bare, nude, unclothed, undressed, in one's birthday suit (*informal*), in the buff (*informal*)

name n. *I've forgotten the name of the book.* designation, heading, title
Ray has a good name in the industry. position, reputation, standing, status

narrow adj. *I have narrow feet.* fine, slender, thin *wide

nasty adj. *What's that nasty smell?* disagreeable, foul, horrible, objectionable, offensive, unpleasant *nice
That was a nasty thing to do to your brother. cruel, hurtful, inconsiderate, malicious, mean, spiteful, unkind *kind

natural adj. *It's only natural that you will ache a little after running a cross-country race.* common, commonplace, expected, ordinary, standard, to be expected, usual *unnatural

naturally adv. *Naturally we will give you your money back if there's a problem.* certainly, clearly, it goes without saying, obviously, of course

nature n. *Ruby has a very sweet nature.* character, disposition, personality, temperament
I watched a really wonderful

program about nature on TV last night. landscape, living world, natural world, outdoors

naughty *adj. The twins are really very naughty at times.* badly behaved, disobedient, disruptive, full of mischief, impish, mischievous, wild, a handful (*informal*) *obedient

near *prep. Sophie lives near the bus station.* adjacent to, bordering on, close to, in the vicinity of

nearly *adv. I've nearly finished reading the last Harry Potter book.* almost, just about, more or less, practically, virtually

neat *adj. I left my books in a neat pile.* orderly, tidy
That's a neat trick! clever, engaging, fun

necessary *adj. It won't be necessary to bring your own equipment; we've got plenty.* called for, compulsory, essential, needed, obligatory, required

need¹ *n. The money we are raising is going to help children and families in need.* deprivation, hardship, poverty

need² *v. I need more time to finish the job.* crave, require, want
I need to speak to the manager. have to, must, ought to, should

negative *adj. Don't make negative comments.* cynical, depressing, gloomy, pessimistic *positive

neglect *v. He bought a puppy, but* *then neglected it.* disregard, fail to care for, ignore, leave unattended, turn one's back on (*informal*) *cherish

neglected *adj. The cottage looks empty and neglected.* abandoned, derelict, dilapidated, ramshackle, tumbledown, uncared for

nerve *n. I didn't have the nerve to volunteer to sing a solo.* bravery, courage, pluck, self-assurance, self-confidence, guts (*informal*)
Natalie had the nerve to say it was my fault that she was late. audacity, gall, impudence

nervous *adj. Emma felt a little nervous before her driving test.* anxious, apprehensive, jumpy, on edge, jittery (*informal*) *calm

neutral *adj. I'm not getting involved in your argument; I'm remaining neutral.* impartial, objective, unbiased, uninvolved, unprejudiced

never *adv. Oliver never eats meat.* at no time, on no occasion, under no circumstances *always

new *adj. Have you seen the new James Bond movie yet?* current, latest, recent, up-to-date *old
Who needs a new notebook? another, different, fresh, unused

news *n. Has there been any news from the hospital?* bulletin, communication, information,

tidings (*literary*)

next¹ *adj. The next class is history.* following, subsequent, succeeding ***last**

next² *prep. I live in the house next to Jenny.* adjacent, adjoining, closest, nearest, neighboring

nice *adj. I hope you have a nice time.* agreeable, enjoyable, pleasant, wonderful ***unpleasant**
We have a very nice couple living next door to us. agreeable, amiable, charming, delightful, friendly, pleasant ***unfriendly**
They live in a nice house. attractive, beautiful, magnificent, splendid ***awful**
If the weather is nice, we'll have a barbecue. fine, pleasant, sunny, warm ***awful**

nod *v. The receptionist nodded when it was my turn to go in and see the doctor.* beckon, indicate, motion, signal

noise *n. The neighbors were making a lot of noise.* din, cacophony, clamor, hubbub, uproar, racket (*informal*) ***silence**

noisy *adj. A crowd of noisy football fans got on the train.* boisterous, loud, rowdy ***quiet**

nonsense *n. Don't talk such nonsense.* balderdash, claptrap, foolishness, drivel (*informal*), garbage (*informal*), trash (*informal*)

normal *adj. The shoes were on sale for half the normal price.* ordinary, regular, standard, typical, usual ***unusual**

nosy *adj. He's so nosy; he always wants to know what everyone is doing.* curious, inquisitive, intrusive, meddlesome, prying, snoopy (*informal*)

notice¹ *n. There's a notice on the wall about the school trip.* announcement, poster, sign

notice² *v. Mark suddenly noticed that he was wearing mismatched socks.* become aware, observe, perceive, see, spot

now *adv. You can start now.* at once, at this moment, immediately, instantly, right away, pronto (*informal*)

Notice

After observing that his bike had a flat tire, Joe knew that he would have to walk to school.

nuisance *n. The train has been delayed; what a nuisance!* annoyance, bother, inconvenience, problem, drag (*informal*), pain (*informal*)

numb *adj. My toes are numb with cold.* deadened, insensible, lacking sensation, unfeeling

number *n. We've received a large number of replies.* amount, quantity, sum

Oo

obedient *adj. Our dog isn't very obedient; he behaves terribly.* compliant, deferential, dutiful, respectful, well disciplined ***naughty**

obey *v. Drivers must obey the rules of the road.* abide by, adhere to, comply with, conform to, observe, stick to, submit to ***disobey**

object[1] *n. (**ob**-ject) Harry dusted the objects on the shelf.* article, item, thing
The object of the game of chess is to take your opponent's king. aim, goal, intention, objective, purpose

object[2] *v. (ub-**ject**) Many residents objected to the new tax proposal.* be against, complain about, disagree with, disapprove of, oppose, protest

against ***approve**

obscure[1] *v. Low clouds obscured our view of the eclipse.* conceal, cover, hide, mask, veil ***reveal**

obscure[2] *adj. There are too many obscure words in the crossword puzzle.* confusing, difficult, incomprehensible, puzzling, specialized, unknown ***clear**

obstacle *n. The new law is an obstacle to progress.* bar, barrier, hindrance, hurdle, obstruction, stumbling block ***benefit**

obstinate *adj. Some politicians are so obstinate; they simply won't listen to other people's views.* headstrong, stubborn, tenacious, uncompromising, unyielding

obstruct *v. A truck was obstructing the entrance.* bar, block, clog, close off

obstruction *n. The truck was causing a major obstruction.* barrier, hindrance, hurdle, obstacle, restriction

obvious *adj. It's obvious that you're lying.* apparent, clear, evident, plain, self-evident, staring one in the face (*informal*) ***vague**

occasion *n. I've met him on a number of occasions.* circumstance, event, instance, occurrence, time
Granny's birthday is a special occasion. affair, event, function,

do (*informal*)

occasionally *adv. We occasionally have pizza at school, but not often.* every now and then, from time to time, infrequently, once in a while, on occasion, sometimes ***often**

occupied *adj. This seat is occupied.* engaged, in use, taken, unavailable ***vacant**
Jane's four young children keep her occupied. active, busy, employed, on the go (*informal*) ***idle**

occupy *v. The company occupies two floors of the building.* be based in, be located in, be situated in, inhabit, take up

occur *v. The accident occurred late on Saturday night.* come about, happen, take place, come to pass (*literary*)

odd *adj. All I can find is one odd sock.* lone, remaining, single, solitary, unmatched
There's something very odd about this. bizarre, curious, peculiar, puzzling, strange, weird

off[1] *adj. Aleesha's off today; she's sick.* absent, gone, off duty, on leave, unavailable ***present**

off[2] *adv. I swerved off the road.* away, to the side

offend *v. Tony's comments about her mother offended her deeply.* displease, distress, hurt, hurt

Oceans and Waters

Antarctic Ocean	Bay
Arctic Ocean	Fjord
Atlantic Ocean	Gulf
Indian Ocean	Lagoon
Pacific Ocean	Loch
	Sound
	Strait

the feelings of, insult, upset, wound ***please**

offense *n. Driving too fast is a serious offense.* breach of the law, crime, illegal act, misdeed, unlawful act, violation

offensive *adj. I find those remarks especially offensive.* disrespectful, hurtful, insulting, objectionable, outrageous, rude ***polite**

offer *v. My mom offered to help.* be willing, propose, suggest, volunteer
The church offered their hall to the Scouts for their annual fair. give, make available, provide, put forward, recommend

office *n. My father's construction company has offices in all corners of the world.* agency, branch, bureau, department, division, workspace

official[1] *n. The official checked my bags.* agent, bureaucrat,

clerk, executive, functionary, officer
The official called a penalty.
judge, referee, umpire

official² *adj. A passport is an official document.* authentic, authorized, bona fide, formal, legal, proper ***informal**

often *adv. I don't go to the movies very often.* frequently, generally, habitually, much, regularly, repeatedly ***seldom**

okay *adj. I thought the movie was okay.* all right, fair, passable, reasonable, satisfactory

old *adj. We organized a party for a group of old people.* aged, elderly, mature, senior ***young**
My uncle collects old furniture.
ancient, antique, vintage
***modern**
The library in my old school was much bigger than this one.
earlier, ex-, former, one-time, past, previous ***new**

old-fashioned *adj. Mrs. Donovan wears very old-fashioned clothes.* antiquated, dated, frumpy, outdated, out-of-date
***fashionable**

once *adv. Fleet Street was once the place where all English daily newspapers were published.* at one time, formerly, in the past, previously

only *adv. There are only two tickets left.* just, merely, purely, simply

ooze *v. Blood oozed out from under the bandage.* bleed, discharge, escape, exude, leak, seep, trickle

open¹ *v. Let's open the window since it's so warm.* unfasten, unlock ***close**
I can't wait to open my birthday presents. uncover, undo, unwrap ***wrap**
The movie opens with the violent murder of a diplomat. begin, commence, get under way, start
***end**

open² *adj. The door is open.* ajar, unfastened, unlocked
The government needs to be open about the risks. candid, forthright, frank, honest, outspoken, sincere, up-front
***dishonest**

opening *n. There's an opening in the fence.* crevice, gap, hole, space

operate *v. Do you know how to operate the DVD player?* control, drive, handle, use, utilize, work

operation *n. The soldiers have been involved in peacekeeping operations in the Middle East.* action, activity, affair, procedure, task, undertaking
He was nervous about his upcoming operation.
procedure, surgery

opinion *n. What's your opinion on this matter?* belief, point of

view, standpoint, view, viewpoint

opposite[1] *adj. The presidential candidates have opposite views.* conflicting, contradictory, contrary, opposing

opposite[2] *prep. Ewan lives opposite the swimming pool.* across from, facing

optimistic *adj. I'm pretty optimistic about the future.* cheerful, confident, hopeful, positive, upbeat (*informal*) ***pessimistic**

optional *adj. Spanish is optional at my school.* noncompulsory, up to the individual, voluntary ***compulsory**

order[1] *n. The commander gave orders to shoot the enemy soldiers.* command, decree, directive, instruction, rule
The police were called in to keep order. calm, control, peace, peacefulness ***chaos**

order[2] *v. The judge ordered him to do community service.* command, direct, instruct, require, tell
You can order tickets over the Internet. apply for, book, request, reserve, set aside

ordinary *adj. It's a story about ordinary people.* average, common, regular, standard, typical, usual, run-of-the-mill (*informal*) ***unusual**

organization *n. Lydia works for the organization responsible for preserving old buildings.* agency, association, body, company, establishment, institution, outfit (*informal*)

organize *v. Julie is organizing a party for her parents' anniversary.* arrange, coordinate, plan, set up, sort out ***cancel**

organized *adj. Rachel isn't very organized; she can never find anything on her desk.* businesslike, efficient, methodical, neat, tidy ***messy**

Original

Traveling by camel was a new, novel experience.

origin *n. The origins of the universe go back billions of years.* beginning, birth, dawn, root, source, start *****end**

original *adj. The Picts were the original inhabitants of Scotland.* earliest, first, indigenous, initial *****last**

The artist's work is interesting and original. avant-garde, groundbreaking, imaginative, innovative, new, novel *****typical**

other *adj. Are there any other books about the French Revolution in the library?* additional, alternative, different, extra, further, more

out *adj. I'm afraid that Mr. Lucas is out at the moment.* absent, away, elsewhere, unavailable

outing *n. The school outing is next Wednesday.* day out, excursion, expedition, field trip, trip

outline *n. Molly drew the outline of a flower in pencil.* diagram, shape, sketch

Before you start to write your story, it's a good idea to make an outline of the main ideas. abstract, framework, plan, summary, synopsis

out of order *adj. The escalator is out of order.* broken, defective, faulty, inoperative, not working, out of service

outside *adj. Dad is painting the outside walls of the house.* exterior, external, outdoor, outer

over¹ *adv. The football game will be over in five minutes.* at the end, concluded, ended, finished

over² *prep. Look at the clouds over the mountains.* above, beyond, overhead

owe *v. Jamie owes a large amount of money to some dangerous people.* be in debt to, be obliged for, be in the red (*informal*)

own¹ *v. I don't own a car, but I do have a bicycle.* have, hold, possess *****lack**

own² *adj. My sister wants to buy her own apartment.* individual, personal, private

own up *v. If no one is prepared to own up, then you will all stay behind after school.* accept responsibility, accept the blame, admit, confess, come clean (*informal*)

Pp

pack¹ *n. The museum provides an information pack for visitors.* bundle, collection, packet, set

pack² *v. Grace packed all of her things into a suitcase.* cram, fill, load, stuff

packed *adj.* *The stores were packed.* busy, crowded, full, overcrowded *****empty**

pain *n.* *I've got a pain in my side.* ache, cramp, pang, spasm, stitch, twinge
The game has been canceled; what a pain! bother, inconvenience, nuisance, drag (*informal*), pain in the neck (*informal*)
Callum is a real pain. nuisance, pest, pain in the neck (*informal*)

painful *adj.* *A cold sore can sometimes be very painful.* aching, agonizing, excruciating, sore, tender
It was painful to watch the baby get a shot. emotional, heartbreaking, sad

pale *adj.* *Toby looks a little pale today.* ashen, colorless, pasty, wan (*literary*) *****healthy**
I prefer pale colors to dark ones. faint, light, muted, pastel, soft *****bright**

pamper *v.* *My mother loves to be pampered in spas.* baby, humor, indulge, spoil

pan *n.* *You need to put the mushrooms into the pan.* container, frying pan, pot, saucepan, wok

panic¹ *n.* *Hundreds of people ran from their homes in panic when the tsunami struck.* alarm, fear, fright, terror

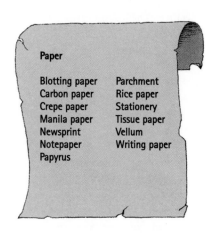

Paper

Blotting paper	Parchment
Carbon paper	Rice paper
Crepe paper	Stationery
Manila paper	Tissue paper
Newsprint	Vellum
Notepaper	Writing paper
Papyrus	

panic² *v.* *People started to panic when the lights went out.* be afraid, be alarmed, become hysterical, be frightened, be scared, lose control, fall to pieces (*informal*) *****relax**

pant *v.* *I was panting after running for the bus.* be breathless, gasp, huff and puff (*informal*)

parade¹ *n.* *The Brownies and Cub Scouts took part in the parade.* display, march, pageant, procession

parade² *v.* *She paraded around the office wearing her new shoes.* march, show off, strut

part¹ *n.* *All of the different parts of the camera are labeled in the instruction booklet.* accessory, attachment, constituent, element, piece, portion, section
The program is in three parts.

episode, installment, section
The old part of town is considered upper class. area, district, neighborhood, quarter, region, sector, zone
Charlotte is playing the part of the mother. character, role

part² *v. The curtains parted, and the dancers came onstage.*
divide, open, separate ***close**

particular *adj. If you want to work in a particular department, say so on your application form.*
definite, distinct, individual, special, specific
Adam is very particular about his appearance. choosy, fastidious, finicky, fussy, meticulous ***careless**

partly *adv. We won the soccer game partly because the other team was down to only ten men.*
in part, partially, to a certain extent, to some degree, up to a point

partner *n. You'll need a partner for this exercise.* ally, associate, colleague, companion, coworker, helper

party *n. The party was held in a hotel.* celebration, festivity, function, gathering, get-together, reception, social, social gathering, bash (*informal*), do (*informal*)

pass¹ *n. You need a pass to get in.*
permit, ticket, warrant

pass² *v. Please pass me the salt.*

give, hand, hand over
As I passed the police officer, he looked at me suspiciously. catch up, go ahead of, outstrip, overtake
Four weeks passed. elapse, go by, slip by
Hannah passed her driving test. be successful in, get through, qualify, succeed in ***fail**

past *adj. I've read so many books in the past few weeks.* last, recent ***next**

path *n. There was a path leading down to the beach.* footpath, track, trail, walkway

pathetic *adj. That's a really pathetic joke.* feeble, poor, weak, hopeless (*informal*) ***great**

Paths and Passageways

Alley	Mountain pass
Avenue	Passage
Boulevard	Path
Drive	Road
Freeway	Sidewalk
Highway	Street
Lane	Thoroughfare

patient *adj. Be patient and wait your turn.* calm, even-tempered, long-suffering, tolerant, understanding, forbearing (*formal*) ***impatient**

patrol *v. Soldiers patrolled the downtown area.* guard, keep a lookout, keep watch, police, stand guard

pattern *n. The frost has made a delicate pattern on my bedroom window.* arrangement, decoration, design, motif

pause¹ *n. There was a short pause in the speech.* adjournment, break, intermission, interruption, interval, lull, rest, breather (*informal*)

pause² *v. We'll pause for some refreshments.* adjourn, break (off), cease, have a break, stop, take a break, take a breather (*informal*) ***continue**
She paused before replying to the question. delay, falter, hesitate, wait

pay¹ *n. The strikers want a raise in pay.* earnings, remuneration, salary, wages

pay² *v. Mr. Ali paid me for washing his car.* recompense, remunerate, reward
We paid $10 to get into the game. give, spend, cough up (*informal*), fork out (*informal*), lay out (*informal*), shell out (*informal*)

pay for *v. A local company paid for the team's soccer uniforms.* donate, finance, sponsor, subsidize
"You'll pay for this," he threatened. be punished, suffer, suffer the consequences, get one's just desserts (*informal*)

pay off *v. All of Keira's hard work has paid off.* be successful, bring success, get results, have an effect, work ***fail**

peace *n. I love the peace and quiet of the countryside.* calm, calmness, quiet, quietness, stillness, tranquillity ***noise**
The congregation prayed for world peace. end of hostilities, friendship, harmony, nonviolence, reconciliation ***war**

peaceful *adj. The new hotel is situated in a peaceful valley.* calm, quiet, restful, sleepy, tranquil ***noisy**

peculiar *adj. This chocolate tastes peculiar.* bizarre, odd, strange, weird

people *n. The streets were crowded with people doing their Christmas shopping.* citizens, human beings, humans, public, residents, folks (*informal*)

perfect *adj. Lizzie's spelling is always perfect.* excellent, faultless, flawless, ideal, impeccable, without fault ***faulty**

perform v. *After you've read the instructions, you'll be able to perform the task.* accomplish, achieve, carry out, complete, do, fulfill
The school is performing Grease *this year.* act, present, produce, put on, stage

perfume n. *These roses give off a lovely perfume.* aroma, fragrance, odor, scent, smell

perhaps adv. *Will you be at the meeting this evening? Perhaps.* maybe, possibly

period n. *The period between the world wars was difficult for Europe.* age, decade, epoch, era, time
We had more than ten inches of rain over a period of two days. duration, interval, space, span, spell, time

permanent adj. *Zak is finding it difficult to secure a permanent job.* fixed, long-term, secure, stable *temporary
Failure to obey the rules may result in a permanent ban on Internet use. enduring, everlasting, indefinite, lasting, lifelong *temporary

permission n. *Your parents must give their permission.* agreement, approval, authorization, consent, sanction

person n. *He's a very strange person.* human being, individual

personal adj. *Take care of your personal belongings.* individual, own, particular, private *joint
Please don't look at my diary; it's personal. confidential, intimate, private, secret *public
The band made a personal appearance. actual, live, in the flesh (*informal*)

personality n. *Shannon is known for her easygoing personality.* character, disposition, nature, temperament

persuade v. *I'm trying hard to persuade my parents to buy a kitten.* cajole, coax, convince, encourage, induce, influence, talk into, urge

pessimistic adj. *Charlie has a pessimistic view of the future of the planet.* cynical, defeatist, dismal, gloomy, negative *optimistic

pest n. *My little brother can be a total pest at times.* bother, menace, nuisance, pain (*informal*)

pester v. *Jodie kept pestering her sister.* annoy, badger, bother, harass, hassle (*informal*)

pet¹ n. *Dorian is the teacher's pet.* beloved, darling, favorite
We have five pets. animal, creature, domestic animal

pet² v. *She pets the cat.* rub, stroke, touch

petty adj. *There are too many petty rules.* minor, trifling,

trivial, unimportant ***important**

phrase *n. What does the phrase "read between the lines" mean?* expression, idiom, saying, sentence, turn of phrase

physical *adj. The physical world includes everything around you that you can see and touch.* actual, concrete, material, real, solid, substantial
You need good physical fitness to join the army. bodily, corporal, corporeal, personal
The game began to get quite physical. tough, vicious, vigorous, violent

pick *v. Pick the one you want.* choose, decide on, opt for, select, settle on, single out
Sam picked some flowers for his mom. collect, gather, pluck

pick on *v. The other children are always picking on Leo.* bully, goad, tease, torment

picture *n. There are pictures on all of the walls.* canvas, drawing, illustration, painting, portrait, print

piece *n. He ate a large piece of chocolate.* block, chunk, hunk, lump, slab, square
The bird ate a small piece of bread. crumb, morsel, slice, sliver
She used a piece of material. bit, fragment, remnant, sample, scrap

pierce *v. Pierce the meat with a skewer before you start cooking it.* penetrate, perforate, prick, puncture, stab

pile *n. There was a pile of clothes on the floor.* heap, jumble, mass, mound, stack

pile up *v. The books will pile up until he shelves them.* accumulate, gather, make a mess

pimple *n. I've got a pimple on my nose.* blemish, zit (*informal*)

pin *v. The teacher pinned the test results to the notice board.* attach, fasten, fix, staple, tack ***undo**

pinch *v. Ow! Susie pinched my arm.* nip, squeeze, tweak

pine *v. I spent my vacation pining*

Pine

The flowers in the pot are wasting away from lack of water.

for my dog. hanker (after), long, miss, yearn

The elderly man seemed to be pining away. decline, languish, lose strength, waste away, weaken

pipe *n. The pipes are under the floorboards.* conduit, duct, hose, tube

pit *n. We dug a pit to bury our trash.* crater, ditch, hole, hollow, trench

pity[1] *n. I feel pity when I see homeless people.* compassion, sadness, sorrow, sympathy, tenderness

pity[2] *v. I pity people who have to work nights.* be sympathetic toward, feel sorry for, grieve for, sympathize with

place[1] *n. This is a good place for a picnic.* locale, location, position, site, spot, venue
Which places have you visited? area, country, region
I'd like a place of my own. apartment, home, house, property
Is this place taken? chair, seat, space

place[2] *v. Place the magazines back onto the shelf.* arrange, deposit, lay, position, put, set down

plain[1] *adj. I'm wearing a plain T-shirt and jeans.* ordinary, simple, unadorned, unpatterned
***fancy**
It's quite plain that you haven't

read the book. apparent, clear, evident, obvious, self-evident

plain[2] *adv. (informal)*
Skateboarding without a helmet is plain stupid. absolutely, completely, downright, utterly, very

plan[1] *n. The architect brought along the plans for the building.* blueprint, chart, design, diagram, drawing, sketch
The plan is to meet outside the theater. aim, arrangement, decision, idea, intention, suggestion

plan[2] *v. I'm going to plan my story before I start writing anything.* design, draft, figure out, organize, prepare
What are you planning to do this weekend? aim, expect, have in mind, hope, intend, mean to do
I need to plan my summer vacation to the Caribbean. arrange, organize, prepare for, think about

plant *v. You should plant seeds now if you want flowers in the summer.* scatter, sow

play *v. The little children were playing in the yard.* frisk, frolic, romp
Our school is playing Saint Matthew's on Saturday. challenge, compete against, take on

playful *adj. Our new kitty is very*

Planets

The eight main planets of our solar system, plus a dwarf planet named Pluto, travel around a star that we call the Sun.

Earth
Jupiter
Mars
Mercury
Neptune
Pluto
Saturn
Uranus
Venus

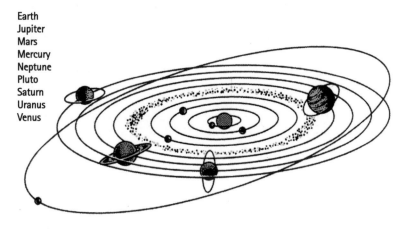

playful. energetic, frisky, high-spirited, impish, lively ***serious**

pleasant *adj. My dentist is a very pleasant man.* affable, agreeable, charming, cheerful, genial, personable ***unpleasant**
We've had a very pleasant evening. agreeable, delightful, enjoyable, entertaining ***boring**

please *v. It's very hard to please Mrs. Griffiths; she's quite fussy.* delight, gratify, keep happy, satisfy ***upset**

pleased *adj. I was very pleased with all of the birthday presents that I received.* content, delighted, glad, gratified, happy, satisfied, thrilled ***disappointed**

pleasure *n. It gives me great pleasure to be able to attend today.* delight, enjoyment, happiness, joy, satisfaction ***sadness**

plenty *n. There are plenty of spoons in the drawer.* a large number, a lot, an abundance, enough, lots, more than enough ***few**

plot¹ *n. The movie has a good plot.* narrative, story, story line
The spies hatched a plot. conspiracy, intrigue, plan, scheme
The garden is on a good plot of land. area, piece, section

plot² *v. Edward and his brother are plotting a surprise party for their sister.* arrange, hatch, organize, plan

plug *v. The plumber plugged the leak with a temporary sealant.* block, cork, seal
The actor went on the talk show only to plug his new movie. (*informal*) advertise, boost, draw attention to, promote, publicize

plump *adj. She's very plump.* chubby, fat, overweight, round, pudgy (*informal*), tubby (*informal*) *thin

plunge *v. Nina plunged into the water.* dive, jump, leap

point¹ *n. The tool has a sharp point.* barb, end, prong, spike, tip
What are the main points of the story? aspect, detail, element, fact, factor, idea, issue, topic
I fell asleep at one point. moment, period, stage, time
I don't see the point of doing this. advantage, aim, object, purpose, reason, use

point² *v. The cowboy pointed his gun at the sheriff.* aim, direct, level

pointless *adj. I used to think that physics was a pointless subject.* absurd, meaningless, senseless, silly, useless, vague *important

point out *v. He pointed out why we should stay in New York for Thanksgiving.* explain, reason, show, suggest

poisonous *adj. Don't touch those berries; they might be poisonous.* deadly, harmful, lethal, noxious, toxic *safe

poke *v. Leon poked me in the ribs.* dig, elbow, jab, nudge, prod, push

pole *n. The dancers attached ribbons to the pole and danced around it.* pillar, post, rod, stake, stick

polish *v. The cadets polished their shoes.* buff, clean, rub, shine, burnish (*literary*)

polite *adj. The children in this school are very polite.* civil, courteous, gracious, respectful, well-bred, well-mannered *rude

pollute *v. The factory had been polluting the river.* adulterate, contaminate, poison, taint

pool¹ *n. There's a small pool of water behind the rock.* pond, puddle
India has a large pool of skilled graduates. accumulation, reserve, stock, supply

pool² *v. We all pooled our cash so that we could buy a large pizza.* amalgamate, combine, contribute, share

poor *adj. The charity helps poor people.* destitute, impoverished, needy, penniless, poverty-stricken, broke (*informal*) *rich
I got a poor grade on my test. bad, awful, third-rate, unacceptable, unsatisfactory *excellent
You've got a cold? You poor

thing! luckless, pitiable, pitiful, unfortunate, unlucky *****fortunate**

poorly *adv. The website is poorly designed and hard to use.* badly, imperfectly, inexpertly, shoddily *****well**

pop *v. The balloon popped.* bang, burst, crack, explode

popular *adj. Tyler is one of the most popular members of the class.* admired, favorite, in demand, in favor, preferred, sought after, well liked *****unpopular**

Jack is a very popular boy's name. common, current, fashionable, prevalent, typical, widespread *****unusual**

portion *n. Mel asked for a small portion of mashed potatoes.* amount, helping, quantity, serving

position *n. This is the position on the map.* bearings, location, place, site, situation, spot, whereabouts

People often pray in a kneeling position. pose, posture, stance

positive *adj. Are you positive that it was Jason you saw?* certain, confident, definite, sure

We got positive feedback from the participants. constructive, enthusiastic, favorable, good, helpful, useful *****negative**

possessions *n. pl. Make sure to keep an eye on your possessions.* belongings, property, things, personal effects (*formal*)

possible *adj. Sorry, I can't do it; it's just not possible.* achievable, feasible, practical, viable

It's possible that I may have to go away. conceivable, imaginable, likely, probable, in the cards (*informal*) *****impossible**

postpone *v. The meeting has been postponed until next week.* adjourn, defer, delay, put off, reschedule (for) *****arrange**

pot *n. Put the water in a pot.* basin, bowl, container, jar, pan, vessel

Poisonous Plants

Aconite
Baneberry
Belladonna
Black nightshade
Cowslip
Deadly nightshade
Ergot
Foxglove
Hellebore
Hemlock
Henbane
Larkspur
Milkweed
Moonseed
Nux vomica
Oleander
Poison ivy
Saint John's
  wort
Wisteria

pour v. *Water poured over the edge of the bathtub.* cascade, flow, gush, jet, spill, spout, stream, surge

poverty n. *There are too many people living in poverty.* deprivation, hardship, need *wealth

power n. *The police have the power to stop a vehicle.* ability, authority, right
The opposition wants to reduce the power of the president. authority, command, control, influence, clout (*informal*)
Scientists underestimated the power of the earthquake. energy, force, might, strength

powerful adj. *A powerful storm is due any day.* forceful, mighty, strong, vigorous, violent *weak
Powerful people head that company. dominant, high-powered, important, influential, potent *minor

practical adj. *The bag looks very attractive, but it's not at all practical, is it?* functional, sensible, suitable, useful *useless
I'll be gaining practical experience in a hospital. actual, applied, hands-on

practice¹ n. *It's common practice to see a nurse rather than a doctor.* custom, habit, policy, procedure, routine
There'll be a practice after school tonight. rehearsal, run-through, training session, dry run (*informal*)

practice² v. *You need to practice your scales if you want to be a good pianist.* do, perfect, rehearse, repeat, run through, study, work at/on

praise v. *The police praised the boys for their quick thinking.* acclaim, applaud, commend, compliment, congratulate, pay tribute to, speak highly of *criticize

precious adj. *Some precious stones are rare.* costly, expensive, priceless, valuable *cheap
My teddy bear is one of my most precious possessions. cherished, dear, favorite, prized, treasured, valued

precise adj. *The map shows the precise location of our office.* accurate, correct, exact, right, specific *approximate

predict v. *I can't predict the future.* divine, forecast, foresee, foretell, prophesy

prefer v. *Which of these delicious cakes would you prefer?* choose, favor, incline toward, like better, select, want

prejudice n. *The aim of our organization is to bring an end to all types of prejudice.* bias, bigotry, discrimination, intolerance

prejudiced *adj. Some people hold very prejudiced views without realizing it.* biased, bigoted, intolerant, narrow-minded, one-sided, partisan

prepare *v. The restaurant manager asked Freya to prepare a business plan.* draft, draw up, design, develop, formulate, produce
The schoolchildren are busy preparing for the mayor's visit. get ready, make arrangements, make preparations, practice, rehearse

present[1] *n.* (*prez-ent*) *Dan received a lot of graduation presents this year.* contribution, donation, gift

present[2] *v.* (*pre-zent*) *The mayor presented the prizes.* award, bestow, confer, distribute, give, hand out

present[3] *adj.* (*prez-ent*) *Everyone is present.* available, here, in attendance *absent

preserve *v. We must preserve the natural environment.* care for, conserve, keep, look after, protect, safeguard, take care of *neglect

press *v. Press the button.* bear down on, compress, depress, flatten, hold down, push (down on), touch *pull

pretend *v. The reporter pretended to be an Arab sheik.* claim, impersonate, masquerade as, profess

pretty *adj. My sister is very pretty.* attractive, beautiful, exquisite, gorgeous, lovely, stunning *ugly
They live in a pretty village. charming, delightful, picturesque, pleasant, quaint, scenic *ugly

prevent *v. Unfortunately we cannot prevent hurricanes.* avert, forestall, put a stop to, stop, thwart, ward off *allow

previous *adj. I'd already met her on a previous occasion.* earlier, former, prior *next

price *n. Prices have gone up.* charge, cost, fee, payment, rate

prick *v. I pricked my finger on a thorn.* jab, pierce, puncture, stab

pride *n. Elliot takes such pride in his work.* delight, pleasure, satisfaction
Pride is one of the seven deadly sins. arrogance, conceit, egotism, self-importance, vanity

principle *n. The course covers the basic principles of medicine.* guideline, law, regulation, rule, standard
I'm not going to lie to my mother; I still have my principles. belief, code of honor, integrity, morals, standards

print *v. We printed 1,000 copies of the leaflet.* circulate, disseminate, issue, produce, publish

private *adj. This is a private meeting; only those invited are allowed to attend.* confidential, exclusive, nonpublic, secret
*public
Let's find a private place where we can chat without anyone interrupting. isolated, quiet, remote, secluded, undisturbed, out of the way (*informal*)
*crowded

prize *n. Scott won a prize in the talent contest.* award, honor, reward, trophy

probably *adv. I'll probably catch the six o'clock bus.* almost certainly, doubtless, in all likelihood, more than likely

problem *n. Max has some financial problems.* complication, difficulty, worry, headache (*informal*)

produce *v. Hal's company produces patio furniture.* assemble, construct, create, make, manufacture, put together ***destroy**
The president's speech produced an enthusiastic response. bring about, cause, engender, give rise to, result in

professional *adj. Professional athletes, such as football players, are often paid very well.* nonamateur, paid, salaried
The ad says that the apartment would suit a professional person. executive, white-collar

Typewritten letters look much more professional. businesslike, efficient, polished, skilled
*amateur

profit *n. The summer festival made a profit of $500.* benefit, gain, income, proceeds, return, takings, yield

progress *n. There has been some progress in the campaign over the past week.* advancement, development, growth, headway, improvement, progression

promise[1] *n. I never break my promises.* assurance, commitment, pledge, undertaking, word of honor
Aaron shows promise on the football field. ability, potential, talent

promise[2] *v. Will you promise never to do that again?* agree, give one's word, guarantee, pledge, swear, vow

promote *v. My mom has just been promoted at work.* elevate, give a promotion to, upgrade
The government campaign promotes healthy eating. back, encourage, endorse, foster, recommend, support
He agreed to be on the news program only so that he could promote his new book. advertise, publicize, hype (*informal*), plug (*informal*)

promptly *adv. They arrived promptly.* in good time, on time,

punctually, on the dot
(*informal*) ***late**
proof *n. Do you have any proof
that Jonathan and David took
your cell phone?* confirmation,
evidence, facts
proper *adj. I don't know the
proper way to eat an artichoke.*
accepted, accurate, correct,
right, usual ***wrong**
property *n. Stolen property was
found in the house.* belongings,
goods, possessions, things
*This drug has similar properties
to aspirin.* attribute,
characteristic, feature, quality
prospect *n. There's no prospect of
the weather improving before the
weekend.* chance, expectation,
forecast, likelihood, possibility
protect *v. The animals protected
their young.* defend, guard, keep
safe, secure, watch over ***attack**
proud *adj. Omar's parents were
very proud as he walked onstage
to get his award.* delighted,
happy, pleased, thrilled
***ashamed**
*He is too proud to admit that he
is wrong.* arrogant,
condescending, haughty,
supercilious, vain ***modest**
prove *v. Can you prove that this is
your car?* demonstrate,
establish, provide evidence,
provide proof, show
provide *v. Would you believe
that we have to provide our own*

uniform? bring, contribute,
furnish, supply
prowl *v. I think there's someone
prowling around outside.* creep,
lurk, roam, skulk
pry *v. Sammy is always prying
into other people's business.*
interfere, intrude, meddle,
snoop, spy (on)
public[1] *n. The public has a right
to know what the government
does in its name.* citizens,
people, population, society
public[2] *adj. Public libraries
abound in this city.* civil,
communal, community,
government, municipal,
national, social, state ***private**
publish *v. The company publishes
dozens of magazines.* bring out,
circulate, distribute, issue, print,
produce
puff *v.* (*informal*) *I was puffing
loudly by the time I reached the
top of the hill.* be breathless,
gasp, pant, wheeze, huff and
puff (*informal*)
pull *v. The horse was pulling a
heavy cart.* drag, draw, haul,
tow ***push**
punch *v. The player was so angry
at being called for a foul that he
punched the referee.* beat, hit,
pound, pummel, strike
punctual *adj. The ferry was
punctual.* on schedule, on time,
prompt ***late**
punish *v. The teacher punished*

Matt. chastize, discipline, penalize, scold, make an example of (*informal*) ***let off**

pure *adj. This sweater is made of pure wool.* genuine, real ***artificial**

Breathe in the pure mountain air. clean, clear, fresh, germfree, natural, unpolluted ***unhealthy**

purpose *n. The purpose of a dictionary is to define words.* aim, function, goal, intention, point, reason, role

push *v. Push the door.* bear down on, compress, depress, flatten, hold down, press ***pull**

One of the other passengers in the line was pushing me. bump, elbow, jostle, nudge, poke, press against, shove

put *v. Put your clothes in the closet.* hang, leave, place

Put the books on the shelf. lay, pile, place, stack, stand

He put his football uniform into his bag. place, shove (*informal*), stick (*informal*)

She put salt on her fries. pour, sprinkle

He put his hockey stick against the wall. lean, prop, rest, stand

She put money into her bank account. deposit, pay in, place

put back *v. Please put the book back on the shelf.* put away, replace, return

put down *v. My boss is always putting me down.* belittle, criticize, disparage, humiliate ***praise**

The army put down the revolt. crush, defeat, quash, suppress

put off *v. The game has been put off till next month.* adjourn, defer, delay, postpone, reschedule (for) ***arrange**

She was put off by his bad manners. repel (by), repulse (by)

put up with *v. I'm not going to put up with this behavior any longer.* accept, endure, stand for, tolerate

puzzle *n. The meaning of the stone circle at Stonehenge has always been a puzzle.* enigma, mystery, riddle

puzzled *adj. Anita looked puzzled by the question.* baffled, bewildered, confused, perplexed

puzzling *adj. His behavior is puzzling.* baffling, bewildering, confusing, curious, incomprehensible, peculiar, strange ***clear**

Qq

quake *v. Taz was quaking with fear.* quiver, shake, shiver, shudder, tremble

qualification *n. You need a qualification to be a teacher.* certificate, degree, diploma, proficiency, skill

qualify *v. People over 60 may qualify for a discount.* be eligible, be entitled (to)

quality *n. People often overlook Nora's good qualities.* attribute, characteristic, feature, trait

I don't think the quality of their products is very good. caliber, condition, grade, standard

quantity *n. A pound of peas is a large quantity.* amount, number, sum, volume, weight

quarrel[1] *n. I could hear that they were having a quarrel.* argument, disagreement, dispute, fight, squabble

quarrel[2] *v. My cousin and I quarrel a lot.* argue, bicker, fight, squabble ***agree**

queen *n. There have been two queens of England named Elizabeth.* head of state, monarch, ruler, sovereign

question *n. Does anyone have any questions?* inquiry, query ***answer**

We need to consider the important question of Internet access. issue, matter, point, problem, subject, topic

quick *adj. That was a very quick journey.* fast, rapid, speedy, swift ***slow**

Auntie Susan paid us a very quick visit. brief, fleeting, short, temporary, whirlwind ***long**

quiet *adj. Be quiet, please; our newborn baby is asleep in the next room.* hushed, noiseless, silent, soundless, speechless ***loud**

These days my aunt lives in a very quiet place. isolated, peaceful, relaxing, sleepy, tranquil ***noisy**

quit *v. He has quit his job.* give up, leave, resign from, step down from ***start**

These patches are supposed to help you quit smoking. discontinue, give up, renounce, stop ***start**

quite *adv. The drama group used to be quite popular with the children.* a bit, fairly, rather, reasonably, slightly, somewhat, to a certain extent, pretty (*informal*)

The word mouse *can have two quite different meanings.* absolutely, altogether, completely, entirely, in every respect, totally

quote *v. My sister quoted what I had said to Mom.* cite, repeat

Rr

raid[1] *n. A man was arrested after the raid.* attack, holdup, robbery

raid² *v. Raccoons raided the house.* descend on, search, swoop in on

rail *n. Hold onto the rail.* banister, railing, rod

rain *n. My party was canceled because of rain.* downpour, precipitation, shower

raise *v. The referee raised his flag.* elevate, hoist, lift (up) *****drop**
The company has raised its prices again. increase, inflate, put up, hike (*informal*), up (*informal*) *****reduce**
We're raising money for charity. collect, get, make, obtain
Could you please raise your voice? amplify, intensify, magnify, make louder

ram *v. The van rammed into the bicyclist.* collide with, crash, drive, slam, smash

random *adj. Investigators believe it was a random attack.* arbitrary, chance, haphazard, indiscriminate, unplanned, unpremeditated

range *n. The store stocks a wide range of sneakers.* assortment, choice, collection, selection, variety
These types of vacations are aimed at young people in the age range of 18–24. extent, limit, parameter, span

rank *n. The police sergeant was promoted to the rank of chief.* class, grade, level, position

rare *adj. It's rare to see you in a skirt, Millie.* atypical, uncommon, unusual, out of the ordinary (*informal*) *****common**
He paid one of his rare visits to his parents. infrequent, occasional, scarce *****usual**

rate¹ *n. I'm not very pleased with the rate of your progress.* pace, speed, tempo
What's the going rate for the condo? charge, cost, payment, price

rate² *v. Visitors are invited to rate how useful they found the website.* appraise, assess, evaluate, grade, put a value on, rank

rather *adv. Would you rather have tea or coffee?* preferably, sooner

rave *v. The teacher was raving about the boy's intellect.* enthuse, sing the praises of (*informal*), wax lyrical (*informal*) *****complain**

raw *adj. This meat is raw.* uncooked, undercooked, underdone
She has raw talent in the sport of hockey. fresh, pure, unabashed

ray *n. A ray of light shone onto the floor.* beam, gleam, shaft, stream
There's a small ray of hope. chance, glimmer, hint, spark

reach *v. It was dark when we reached the campsite.* arrive at,

end up at, get to *leave
*He reached out his hand to take
the money.* extend, hold out,
stretch out, thrust out
*How long will it take me to
reach my target weight of 120
pounds?* achieve, attain, get to,
hit (*informal*)
*I've been trying to reach Tim
all day.* communicate with,
contact, get in contact with,
make contact with, speak to,
get ahold of (*informal*), get in
touch with (*informal*)

react *v. My coworker didn't react
when I told him that I was
resigning.* answer, comment,
reply, respond, show expression

read *v. I enjoy reading books in
the library.* browse (through),
peruse, pore over, study
*It's difficult to read Beth's
handwriting.* decipher, interpret,
make sense of, understand

ready *adj. I'm ready to leave now.*
all set, prepared, set, hyped up
(*informal*)
*Jade is always ready to help
the younger children.* eager,
enthusiastic, happy, pleased,
prepared, willing *reluctant

real *adj. This isn't real fur.*
authentic, bona fide, genuine
*fake
*The hero of the book is based on
a real person.* actual, factual,
nonfictional *imaginary
I've been a real idiot. absolute,

complete, total, utter

realize *v. I realize that it will be
hard to find the time.* appreciate,
be aware, comprehend,
recognize, understand

really *adv. He looks fierce, but
he's really very sweet.* actually,
as a matter of fact, in actual
fact, in fact
I really like him. genuinely,
honestly, sincerely, truly
*I thought the film was really
good.* awfully, exceedingly,
extremely, remarkably, very,
wicked (*informal*)

reason *n. The main reason for the
accident was faulty traffic lights.*
cause, explanation, grounds
*My reason for learning Spanish
is because I'm going to Mexico.*
aim, goal, intention,
motivation, motive, purpose

reasonable *adj. Please be
reasonable and stop arguing.*
rational, sensible *silly
The price is really reasonable.
affordable, cheap, competitive,
fair, inexpensive, moderate,
modest *expensive

rebel *n. (reb-el) The rebels
attacked the village.* guerrilla,
insurgent, resistance fighter,
revolutionary

rebel *v. (re-bel) The sailors on
the Bounty rebelled.* disobey orders,
mutiny, revolt, riot, rise up *obey

rebellious *adj. Brandon was
expelled for being rebellious.*

defiant, disobedient, insubordinate, unruly *obedient

recent *adj. It's a recent movie.* current, modern, new, up-to-date *old

recently *adv. I've been to India recently; it's an amazing country.* a short time ago, lately, not long ago

reckless *adj. Tom is a reckless driver.* careless, heedless, impetuous, irresponsible, rash *cautious

recognize *v. I didn't recognize you.* identify, know, place, recall, recollect, remember
I recognize the seriousness of this problem. accept, acknowledge, appreciate, be aware of, understand

recommend *v. Let's ask the waiter to recommend something.* advise, propose, suggest
The doctor recommended that he stop smoking. advise, advocate, counsel, exhort, suggest, urge

record¹ *n. (**rek**-ord) Do you have a record of the conversation?* account, evidence, file, report, transcript

record² *v. (re-**kord**) All absences of staff must be recorded in the register.* enter, inscribe, log, note, put down, register, write down

recover *v. The police have not yet recovered the stolen goods.* find, reclaim, regain possession of, retrieve, track down *lose
Alex has completely recovered from the accident. bounce back, get back to normal, get better, improve, recuperate, revive

reduce *v. Motorists should try to reduce the number of trips that they make.* curtail, cut back on, decrease, diminish, lessen, scale down *increase
Ticket prices have been reduced. discount, make cheaper, mark down, slash (*informal*) *increase

refer *v. The notice refers only to people who ride the school bus.* affect, apply to, be relevant to, concern
The author refers to her childhood in the book. allude to, broach the subject of, comment on, deal with, mention, remark on, write about *ignore
Refer to your dictionary if there are any words that you don't understand. consult, look up in, use *ignore

referee *n. Referees need to have eyes in the backs of their heads.* adjudicator, arbitrator, judge, linesman, umpire

reference *n. I've already asked my boss to give me a reference.* credentials, recommendation, testimonial

refresh *v. A walk around the block will refresh you.* invigorate,

restore, revive, perk up
(*informal*)

refund *v. If you're not satisfied,
we will refund your money.* pay
back, reimburse, repay, return
*keep

refuse *v. Unfortunately, I had to
refuse the invitation.* decline,
demur, reject, say no to

regard *v. In this school we regard
bullying as a very serious matter.*
consider, look on, view

regret *v. I strongly regret the time
that I got so angry with my
mother.* be ashamed, be sorry,
feel remorse, feel sorry, repent,
rue (*literary*)

regular *adj. Our club holds regular
meetings.* constant, frequent,
periodic ***rare**
*The regular driver was on
vacation.* customary, habitual,
normal, ordinary, standard, usual

reject *v. The workers rejected the
management's offer.* decline,
dismiss, turn down ***accept**

relax *v. Debbie relaxes by sitting
on the garden swing.* rest,
unwind, chill out (*informal*),
take it easy (*informal*)
Relax! We've got plenty of time.
calm down, chill out (*informal*)
*panic

release *v. They released all of
the birds into the wild.* free,
let go, liberate, set free
*imprison

reliable *adj. I'll ask Daisy; she's*

always reliable. dependable,
responsible, sound, trustworthy

relieved *adj. I'm so relieved that
you've finally called; I was worried
about you.* glad, pleased,
reassured, thankful ***worried**

religion *n. There are people of all
different religions here.* belief,
creed, denomination, faith

religious *adj. She is very religious
and wants to be a nun when she
grows up.* devout, pious

reluctant *adj. Reece was reluctant
to lend Josh money.* averse,
disinclined, hesitant, loath,
unwilling ***willing**

rely on *v. You can always rely on
Nancy to help out.* bank on,
count on, depend on, have
confidence in, trust

remain *v. You'll have to remain
here till I come back.* stay, wait,
hang around (*informal*) ***leave**

remainder *n. Who ate the
remainder of the cake?* balance,
remnant, residue, rest, surplus

remark[1] *n. I have to say that I
really don't find that remark
very helpful.* comment,
observation, statement,
utterance

remark[2] *v. "That's a very ugly
dog," remarked Holly.*
announce, comment, mention,
observe, point out, say, utter

remarkable *adj. The movie told
the remarkable story of how
penicillin was discovered.*

amazing, astonishing, extraordinary, incredible, marvelous, unbelievable ***ordinary**

remember v. *I can't remember where I put my glasses.* be sure, recall, recollect ***forget**

remind v. *Would you please remind me to buy some stamps?* help remember, prompt
This song always reminds me of my vacation in Jamaica. evoke, take one back to

remove v. *Could you please remove your bags from the table?* get rid of, take away/off
This will remove the stains. clean off, scrape off, scrub off, wash off, wipe off

rent v. *We rented a cottage in France.* hire, lease

repair v. *The mechanic repaired our car.* fix, mend, overhaul, service, patch up (*informal*) ***damage**

repeat v. *I've repeated the page number several times.* recite, reiterate, restate, say again
If you're not careful, you'll have to repeat this grade. do again, duplicate, redo

replace v. *Could you please replace the newspaper when you've finished with it?* put back, restore, return ***keep**
Jed will replace Mick as the manager of the team next season. follow on from,

succeed, supersede, take over from, take the place of

reply[1] n. *Did you ever get a reply from him?* acknowledgment, answer, rejoinder, response, retort

reply[2] v. *He replied briefly to the question.* answer, rejoin, respond, retort

report[1] n. *Simon read out loud his group's report.* account, description, review, statement

report[2] v. *Studies reported a drop in the number of local crimes.* announce, communicate, describe, disclose, make public, reveal

represent v. *In* The Lion, the Witch, and the Wardrobe, *Aslan represents God.* denote, personify, stand for, symbolize
The attack represents an increase in the use of violence by the group. correspond to, denote, depict, illustrate, mean, show

request[1] v. *We can request books that are not in this library.* appeal for, apply for, ask for, order

request[2] n. *We've received a request for a Madonna song.* appeal, desire, wish

require v. *Please e-mail us if you require more details.* desire, need, want, would like
Tap dancing requires a lot of energy. demand, entail, involve, necessitate, need

Rescue

The coast guard came to the aid of the shipwrecked crew.

rescue *v. Troops rescued the hostages.* come to the aid of, liberate, release, save, set free

reserve[1] *n. We'll take a reserve of food with us.* stock, stockpile, store, supply

reserve[2] *v. I've reserved a table in the restaurant for eight o'clock.* arrange, book, order

resign *v. The new secretary has resigned.* leave, step down, quit (*informal*)

resource *n. A thesaurus is always a useful resource for a writer.* aid, benefit, facility, help, support

resources *n. pl. Congo's mineral resources include diamonds and gold.* assets, commodities, raw materials, supplies, wealth

respect[1] *n. You should show respect to your parents.* consideration, courtesy, deference, esteem, politeness ***contempt**

respect[2] *v. I respect all of my teachers.* admire, esteem, have regard for, hold in high esteem, honor, look up to, think highly of

responsible *adj. Corinne is a very responsible girl.* levelheaded, reliable, sensible, trustworthy
The principal severely punished the students who were responsible for the damage. answerable for, at fault, culpable of, guilty of, to blame for ***innocent**
Who's responsible for giving out the homework in this class? accountable for, in charge of, in control of

rest[1] *n. You look tired; get some rest!* relaxation, repose, respite, sleep, time off, tranquillity ***work**
We'll have just one of these chocolates each, and then I'll put the rest in the fridge. extras, others, remainder, remaining ones, surplus

rest[2] *v. The doctor told my mother that she should rest.* relax, repose, take time off, unwind, take it easy (*informal*) ***work**

restless *adj. I'm feeling restless and can't settle down.* agitated, anxious, edgy, fidgety, nervous, on edge, uneasy ***calm**

restore *v. Experts are restoring*

the old furniture. recondition, redo, refurbish, renovate, repair *destroy

result *n. Mistakes are often the result of carelessness.* consequence, effect, outcome *cause

return *v. We returned from our vacation yesterday.* arrive back, come back, get back *leave
I need to return this book to the library as soon as possible. give back, hand back, take back *borrow

reveal *v. The fashion designer revealed her new collection.* display, exhibit, put on display, put on view, show *hide
The media refused to reveal the name of the victim. disclose, divulge, give away, release, say, tell *hide

revenge *n. The ancient Greeks wanted revenge on Troy for the kidnapping of Helen.* reprisal, retaliation, retribution, vengeance

revolting *adj. This soup is absolutely revolting.* disgusting, horrible, nauseating, vile *delicious

rich *adj. If I were rich, I would buy a yacht.* affluent, prosperous, wealthy, well-to-do, loaded (*informal*) *poor

rid, get rid of *v. It's time that I got rid of this old coat.* discard, dispose of, throw away, chuck out (*informal*), scrap (*informal*) *keep

ride *n. Uncle Bill took us for a ride in his new car.* drive, jaunt, journey, outing, trip, spin (*informal*)

ridiculous *adj. That's a ridiculous thing to say!* absurd, crazy, foolish, preposterous, silly *sensible

right¹ *n. You don't have the right to touch my belongings.* power, prerogative, privilege

right² *adj. That's the right answer.* accurate, correct, exact, precise, true *wrong
I'm not wearing the right shoes to go for a long walk. appropriate, correct, ideal, proper, suitable *wrong
It wouldn't be right to take Abdul's phone without asking him. correct, fair, honest, proper *wrong

ring *v. The church bells are ringing.* chime, peal, sound, toll

riot¹ *n. The riot started after the referee disallowed the goal.* commotion, disorder, disturbance, tumult, turmoil, uproar

riot² *v. Students rioted in Paris in 1968.* rampage, rebel, revolt

rip *v. I've ripped my shirt.* tear, split

rise *v. Warm air rises.* ascend, climb, go up *fall
Prices have risen. go up, increase, skyrocket (*informal*) *fall

risk¹ *n. There's an element of risk involved in crossing the street.* chance, danger, hazard, uncertainty

risk² *v. Many poor Africans risk their lives trying to sail to Europe.* endanger, gamble with, jeopardize

river *n. The Shannon is an important river in Ireland.* watercourse, waterway

road *n. The roads are always busy.* avenue, highway, street, thoroughfare

roar *v. The crowd began to roar when the goalkeeper saved the penalty shot.* bellow, cry, shout, yell

rob *v. Men in masks robbed the convenience store yesterday.* break into, burglarize, raid, steal from

Rivers and Waterways

Brook
Canal
Channel
Creek
Lake
Loch
Mere
Pond
Pool
River
Spring
Strait
Stream

rock *v. The boat rocked gently in the wind.* move back and forth, sway, swing, totter

romantic *adj. Jerry has always been very romantic; he buys flowers for his wife every week.* affectionate, amorous, loving, passionate

rotten *adj. The wooden beams in the house are completely rotten.* crumbling, decaying, decomposing, disintegrating
The meat in the fridge is rotten. bad, moldy, putrid, rancid *fresh
I feel rotten; I think I'm getting the flu. (*informal*) bad, off-color, sick, unwell, lousy (*informal*), under the weather (*informal*) *well

rough *adj. We walked along a rough track.* bumpy, rocky, stony, uneven *smooth
The sea in the English Channel was very rough. agitated, choppy, turbulent *calm
Tweed has a fairly rough texture. coarse, scratchy *smooth
That's a rough neighborhood— be careful there. aggressive, belligerent, boisterous, rowdy, unruly *gentle
I'll do a rough copy of my homework first. crude, draft, preliminary *perfect
Give me a rough idea of how many people will be there. approximate, estimated, general, vague, ballpark (*informal*) *exact

routine¹ *n. Babies always seem to*

prefer a fixed routine. practice, procedure, regimen, schedule, system

routine² *adj. I'm going to the dentist tomorrow for a routine checkup.* normal, ordinary, regular, standard *****unusual**

row *n. They were standing in a row.* column, file, line, queue, string

rowdy *adj. There was a very rowdy gang in the park.* boisterous, disruptive, riotous, rough, unruly *****quiet**

rub *v. Will you rub my back?* knead, massage, stroke
Amber rubbed sunscreen on her skin. apply, put on, smear, spread

rude *adj. The person who answered the phone was very rude.* abusive, boorish, discourteous, disrespectful, ill-mannered, impertinent, impolite, impudent, insolent, sassy (*informal*) *****polite**

ruin¹ *n. They've let the castle fall into ruin.* decay, disintegration, disrepair

ruin² *v. The red wine ruined the carpet.* damage, destroy, make a mess of, mess up, spoil, wreck

rule¹ *n. The students think that there are too many school rules.* directive, law, regulation

rule² *v. Queen Elizabeth I ruled England from 1558 to 1603.* control, direct, govern, lead, manage, reign

ruler *n. Cleopatra was the ruler of*

Rulers, Monarchs, and Leaders

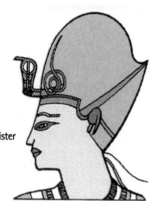

Caesar
Czar
Czarina
Emperor
Empress
King
Mikado
Mogul
Pharaoh
President
Prime Minister
Prince
Princess
Queen
Rajah
Sultan

the ancient Egyptians. chief, head of state, king, leader, monarch, queen, sovereign

rumor *n. There's a rumor going around that the college building might be sold next year.* gossip, hearsay, speculation, tittle-tattle (*informal*)

run *v. The boy ran with great speed down the road.* dash, hasten, hurry, speed, sprint, tear (*informal*)
Nell runs her own business. administer, be in charge of, manage, own

run away *v. The boys rang the bell and then ran away.* bolt, leg it (*informal*), make a run for it (*informal*), skedaddle (*informal*) *****arrive**

rush *v. Ginger rushed into her office.* dart, dash, hurry, run *****dawdle**

Ss

sad *adj. Erin is sad because her cat died.* depressed, despondent, gloomy, heartbroken, melancholy, miserable, unhappy, upset ***happy**
It was a very sad movie. depressing, distressing, harrowing, heartbreaking, tragic, upsetting ***happy**

sadness *n. There was a look of real sadness in her eyes.* despair, despondency, grief, sorrow, unhappiness, woe ***happiness**

safe *adj. The missing children were found safe at a friend's house.* out of danger, unharmed, unhurt ***hurt**
You must always make sure to keep guns in a safe place. secure, well protected ***dangerous**
Is this ladder safe? secure, sound, sturdy ***dangerous**
The medicine is safe for children. benign, harmless, innocuous, nontoxic ***poisonous**
My mom is a very safe driver. careful, cautious ***reckless**

safety *n. Seat belts are provided for the safety of passengers.* protection, security, welfare, well-being ***danger**
Victims are taken to a place of safety. protection, refuge, sanctuary, shelter ***danger**

sag *v. The mattress sags in the middle.* curve, droop, hang down

salary *n. Russell's salary is very low.* income, pay, remuneration, wages

same *adj. Martha and Jessica have the same bag.* identical, matching, similar ***different**

sarcastic *adj. My boss made a sarcastic comment when I arrived late.* cutting, ironic, sardonic

satisfaction *n. She looked at her*

Sacred Books

Apocrypha
Bhagavad-Gita
Bible
Book of Common Prayer
Book of Mormon
Granth
Koran
Rig-Veda
Talmud
Torah
Tripitaka
Upanishad

garden with satisfaction.
contentment, delight, pride

satisfactory adj. A C grade on the test means satisfactory. acceptable, adequate, fair, good enough, passable, reasonable

satisfied adj. I'm satisfied with the grade I got. content, happy, pleased, proud *****disappointed**

save v. The soldiers managed to save all of the hostages. liberate, rescue, set free *****capture**
The newspapers are always telling us to save money and not to spend too much. cut back, economize, scrimp *****spend**

say v. The phrase "this thesaurus" is difficult to say. articulate, pronounce, speak, utter, vocalize
"I'm certainly not doing that," she said. announce, assert, declare, maintain, observe, remark, state
"I think so too," he said. add, answer, rejoin, reply, respond
"Hush," said Annette quietly. "The baby's asleep upstairs." hiss, mouth, murmur, mutter, whisper
"I feel sick; maybe I'm pregnant," said Granny. joke, quip, josh (informal), kid (informal)
"Get off my property at once," he said loudly. bellow, call, cry, exclaim, roar, scream, shout
"Everyone always expects me to do everything," said Mom. complain, grumble, moan, protest, whine (informal)
"Get lost," he said angrily. bark,

snap, snarl
Their website says that they're open on Sundays. communicate, indicate, inform, reveal, show
"Let's say, for the sake of argument, that it will cost $10." assume, estimate, imagine, presume, speculate, suppose

saying n. Look before you leap, as the saying goes. adage, expression, idiom, maxim, motto, phrase, proverb

scale n. Earthquakes are measured on the Richter scale. calibration, measurement
A billionaire is at one end of the scale of wealth, and a beggar is at the other. hierarchy, range, sequence, spectrum
The full scale of the disaster became clear. extent, magnitude, size

scan v. The machine scans the bar code. check, examine, read, scrutinize *****ignore**
Just scan the article quickly and tell me the main points. glance at, read, skim

scandal n. Watergate was an American political scandal that caused President Nixon to resign. impropriety, offense, unethical affair, wrongdoing
It's a scandal that people live on the streets. disgrace, outrage, shame

scarce adj. Water is scarce in many countries. in short supply, lacking, rare, running out *generous

scare v. *You really scared me with that horrible mask!* alarm, frighten, petrify, startle, terrify

scared adj. *My brother's children are scared of the dark.* afraid, frightened, petrified, terrified

scary adj. *That was a really scary movie.* bloodcurdling, frightening, hair-raising, horrifying, spine-chilling, terrifying

scatter v. *The farmer scattered the seeds.* disperse, disseminate, sow, spread, sprinkle
The crowd scattered immediately at the sight of the police horses. break up, disband, disperse *gather

scene n. *We walked by the scene of the crime.* location, place, site, whereabouts
There are cards showing snow scenes. landscape, outlook, picture, view
There was a scene in the movie in which someone was murdered. clip, incident, part, section, snippet

scent n. *These flowers have a lovely scent.* aroma, fragrance, odor, perfume, smell, tang

scope n. *The scope of the project was broad.* breadth, range

score v. *Our team scored ten points.* achieve, attain, gain, record, win *lose

scratch¹ n. *There's a scratch on the paint.* mark, nick, scrape
I've got a small but painful

scratch on my knee. abrasion, cut, graze, wound

scratch² v. *I've scratched my knee.* cut, graze, scrape

scream v. *He was screaming in agony.* bawl, cry, howl, screech, shriek, yell, yelp

scruffy adj. (*informal*) *Tony's clothes are so scruffy.* messy, ragged, shabby, slovenly, tattered *neat

search v. *My parents are still searching for the perfect house.* hunt, look for, seek
Police searched the property. comb, explore, scour

secret adj. *There's a secret panel in the wall.* concealed, disguised, hidden, invisible *obvious
I found his secret diary. classified, confidential, personal, private *public
The spy had secret meetings with his boss. clandestine, covert, undercover *open

section n. *The first section of the book is quite interesting.* chapter, division, part, portion
Melissa works in a different section of our company. branch, department, division, office, sector

secure adj. *What can I do to make my car more secure?* protected, safe, undamaged
Make sure the lid is really secure. closed, fastened, fixed, sealed, sturdy, tight *open

see v. *I can't see the chalkboard.* discern, make out, observe

I saw an interesting TV show.
look at, view, watch
I'll see if Mr. Roberts is in.
ascertain, ask, establish, find out
I don't see the point of this.
appreciate, follow, grasp,
understand

seem *v. He seems to be a really
nice man.* appear, come across
as, look like, sound like

seize *v. The fox seized the chicken
by the throat.* catch, grab, grasp,
snatch, take
*The vice principal seized drug
paraphernalia.* capture,
confiscate, impound, take away

seldom *adv. I seldom go to the
doctor.* almost never, hardly
ever, infrequently, rarely ***often**

select *v. Go to the website and
select the clip you want to see.*
choose, decide on, pick, pick
out, single out

selfish *adj. Don't be selfish; let
me have a piece of candy.*
egotistical, greedy,
inconsiderate, mean, self-
centered ***unselfish**

sell *v. The store sells organic food.*
deal in, market, retail, stock,
trade in, vend ***buy**

send *v. I sent a package to
Canada.* consign, dispatch,
forward, mail

send for *v. The counselor has sent
for you.* call for, request, summon

sense *n. Sawyer had the sense to
cross the street when he saw the
fight starting.* brains, common
sense, intelligence, judgment,
wisdom, gumption *(informal)*
*The word refuse has several different
senses.* definition, gist, meaning

sensible *adj. You should ask Hannah
to help; she's always very sensible.*
down-to-earth, levelheaded,
mature, practical, responsible ***silly**
That's a very sensible decision.
prudent, rational, reasonable,
shrewd, sound, wise ***foolish**

sensitive *adj. She's such a
sensitive child.* easily offended,
easily upset, thin-skinned
(informal), touchy *(informal)*
*Personal hygiene is a very
sensitive issue.* controversial,
delicate, emotive

separate[1] *(sep-e-rit) adj. Our
classroom is in a separate
building.* detached, different,
disconnected, unattached
*same

separate[2] *(sep-e-**rate**) v. The
teacher separated the two boys
who were fighting.* break up,
divide, part, split up ***combine**
Separate the tag from the shirt.
detach, disconnect, disengage,
pull apart, remove ***attach**
*Her parents have recently
separated.* break up, divorce,
get a divorce, part, split up
(informal) ***unite**

series *n. There has been a series of
terrorist attacks on embassies in
recent days.* spate, string, succession

Are you watching the new series on television? program, serial, show, sitcom, soap opera, soap (*informal*)

serious *adj. Why do you always look so serious?* dour, earnest, pensive, solemn, staid, thoughtful

You cannot be serious! earnest, genuine, sincere

This is a very serious matter. critical, grave, important, significant, weighty ***petty**

It was a serious accident. bad, dreadful, major, severe, terrible ***minor**

set[1] *n. I've got a complete set of baseball cards.* collection, group, pack, series

set[2] *v. He set the cup on the table.* deposit, leave, place, put, settle ***take**

The movie is set in Kenya. be located, happen, take place

We haven't set a date for the concert yet. arrange, choose, confirm, decide on, determine, fix, settle on ***cancel**

The gelatin hasn't set yet. congeal, harden, solidify, thicken ***melt**

set[3] *adj. I haven't got a set routine.* established, fixed, standard, strict, usual

I'm dead set on going to the party. determined to, intent on, resolved to

Okay, I'm all set; can we go? prepared, ready, geared up (*informal*)

settle *v. We've tried really hard to settle all of our differences.* reconcile, remedy, resolve, solve, sort out

Settle down, everyone, please . be quiet, calm down, relax

They haven't settled on a date for the wedding yet. arrange, choose, confirm, decide on, determine, fix, set ***cancel**

several *adj. There are several people waiting.* a few, a number of, some, various

severe *adj. There's a severe shortage of water in some places.* critical, dire, grave, serious, worrying ***slight**

The judge said his crime deserved a severe punishment. cruel, harsh, merciless, ruthless, stern, strict

shabby *adj. The furniture is beginning to look shabby.* grubby, neglected, rundown, tattered, scruffy (*informal*) ***elegant**

shake *v. I saw a flash of light, and the ground seemed to shake.* quiver, shudder, tremble, vibrate, wobble

The baby shook the keys. jiggle, rattle, wave

shame *n. She blushed with shame when she remembered what she had done.* disgrace, embarrassment, guilt, humiliation, indignity

The fans have brought shame on their ball club. discredit, disgrace, dishonor, scandal

What a shame you can't come! pity, sad thing, unfortunate situation

shape *n. I could see the shape of the box behind the curtain.* form, outline, structure

share[1] *n. Here's your share of the money we earned.* allocation, helping, part, portion

share[2] *v. Share your candy with your sister, Edward.* divide, split ***keep**

sharp *adj. The knife is very sharp.* penetrating, piercing, pointed
I felt a sharp pain in my side. acute, agonizing, excruciating, intense ***slight**
The sharp student noticed that the teacher had made a mistake. alert, bright, clever, perceptive, quick-witted, smart, on the ball (*informal*)
Cranberry juice has a sharp taste. acidic, sour, strong, tangy, tart

shed[1] *n. My father keeps all of his tools in the shed.* hut, lean-to, shack

shed[2] *v. Some trees shed their leaves during the winter months.* cast off, drop, lose, scatter ***preserve**

shelter[1] *n. The African refugees were given shelter.* accommodation, protection, refuge, sanctuary

shelter[2] *v. The trees sheltered us from the rain.* cover, protect, screen, shield

shine *v. I could see bright lights shining in the distance.* flash, flicker, gleam, glint, glow, sparkle

shiny *adj. The horse that won the race had a really shiny coat.* bright, glossy, polished, sleek ***dull**

shiver *v. The children shivered in the cold.* quiver, shake, shudder, tremble

shock[1] *n. The news about her illness came as a terrible shock to everyone.* blow, surprise, bombshell (*informal*)

shock[2] *v. The brutal murder has shocked the whole community.* appall, daze, horrify, stun, traumatize, upset
I was shocked by her bad language. disgust, horrify, offend, outrage

shocking *adj. It was a shocking event.* appalling, astonishing, awful, disgraceful, outrageous, scandalous ***delightful**

shoot *v. Contestants started shooting their toy guns.* aim, fire

short *adj. She's short and plump.* little, petite, small, squat, stocky, pintsize (*informal*) ***tall**
The newspaper article is quite short. brief, concise, succinct ***long**
Auntie Jane paid a short visit. brief, fleeting, short-lived, temporary ***long**
We're short of bread and milk. deficient in, in need of, lacking in, low on

shortage *n. There has been a shortage of rain in the south this summer.* dearth, deficit, insufficiency, lack, scarcity

shout[1] *n. I heard a shout.* cry, roar, scream, shriek, yell

shout[2] *v. As their boat sank, the fishermen shouted loudly for help.* cry, cry out, roar, scream, shriek, yell

Ships and Boats

Gondola

Kayak

Catamaran

show¹ *n.* *We're putting on a show for the younger children.* concert, performance, production, review, spectacle

show² *v.* *We're going to show the children's pictures in an exhibition.* display, exhibit, put on display, put on view ***hide**

I'll show you how the washing machine works. clarify, demonstrate, explain, illustrate, teach

This shows that the bleach is alkaline. demonstrate, indicate, prove, reveal

Could you please show the next candidate in? bring, escort, guide, invite, lead, take, usher

show off *v.* *Brad is always showing off.* boast, brag, crow, swagger

show up *v.* *How many people bothered to show up?* appear, arrive, come, put in an appearance ***leave**

shrink *v.* *After four weeks the class had shrunk to four people.* contract, diminish, dwindle, reduce ***increase**

shrivel *v.* *The plants shriveled because we forgot to water them.* dry up, shrink, wilt, wither

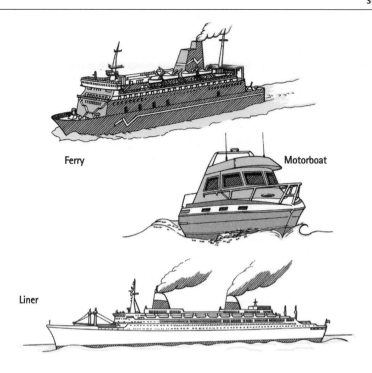

Ferry

Motorboat

Liner

shut *v. Please shut the door.* close, fasten, lock, secure ***open***

shut up *v. (informal) Will you please shut up; I'm trying to study for my test.* be quiet, be silent, keep quiet, hold your tongue *(informal)*, pipe down *(informal)*, put a sock in it *(informal)*, zip it *(informal)* ***speak***

shy *adj. Mo was too shy to raise her hand in front of her classmates.* bashful, embarrassed, meek, nervous, reserved, self-conscious, timid ***confident***

sick *adj. Karl isn't here today; he stayed at home because he is sick.* ill, off-color, unwell, under the weather *(informal)* ***well***
I'm feeling really sick. nauseous, queasy
I'm sick of hearing those people use the same old excuses. bored with, fed up with, tired of, weary of

side *n. In the end, we had a picnic at the side of the road.* border, edge, margin

sigh *v. She looked at the photo and sighed.* breathe out, exhale, respire

sight *n. I have poor sight.*
eyesight, vision
The children laughed at the sight of the clown. appearance, glimpse, view
I'm going to London to see the sights. landmark, place of interest, tourist spot

sign *n. A white flag is an international sign of surrender.* emblem, indication, mark, signal, symbol, token
The spy gave his companion a sign to follow him. gesture, hint, movement, nod, signal
There's a sign saying, "Stay out!" notice, placard, poster, signpost, warning

signal[1] *n. The official gave the signal for the race to start.* cue, gesture, indication, prompt, sign

signal[2] *v. The other driver signaled to me.* beckon, gesture, nod, wave

silence *n. I prefer working in silence.* peace, quiet, stillness, tranquillity ***noise**

silent *adj. The room was silent.* hushed, noiseless, quiet, soundless, still ***noisy**
After Lee berated him, Gary was silent. dumbstruck, lost for words, quiet, speechless ***noisy**

silly *adj. That was a very silly thing to do.* foolish, rash, reckless, senseless, stupid, thoughtless, dumb (*informal*) ***sensible**

similar *adj. Our bags are similar.* alike, almost identical ***different**

simple *adj. I thought the test was simple.* easy, straightforward, a piece of cake (*informal*) ***difficult**
I like simple food. basic, ordinary, plain ***fancy**

sing *v. The birds were singing.* chirp, chirrup, twitter, warble

single *adj. I'd like a single room.* distinct, individual, separate ***joint**

sink *v. The boat sank to the bottom of the sea.* descend, drop, fall ***rise**

sit *v. Sit on that seat over there.* perch, settle down, take a seat, park yourself (*informal*) ***stand up**

site *n. Hopefully, by the end of*

Singers

Alto
Baritone
Bass
Basso profundo
Cantor
Chorister
Contrabass
Contralto
Countertenor
Mezzo-soprano
Prima donna
Soprano
Tenor
Treble
Vocalist

next year this will be the site of the new children's hospital. location, place, setting, situation, spot

situation *n. We found ourselves in a very difficult situation.* case, condition, plight, predicament, state of affairs

size *n. Measure the size of the room.* dimensions, extent, proportions

skill *n. I really admire the skill of glass blowers.* ability, expertise, talent

skillful *adj. The factory is advertising for skillful workers.* able, adept, competent, expert, proficient

skin *n. Some animals are raised for their skin.* coat, fur, hide, pelt *You don't eat the skin of an orange.* peel, rind

slant *v. The kitchen floor slants.* incline, lean, slope, tilt

slap *v. The rider slapped the horse hard in order to make it run faster.* hit, smack, spank, strike, whack (*informal*)

sleep *v. I sometimes sleep for a short while in the afternoons.* doze, nap, rest, catch forty winks (*informal*), snooze (*informal*)

sleepy *adj. I'm feeling sleepy.* drowsy, exhausted, tired, weary ***lively**

slide *v. They slid down the hill on their sled.* glide, slip, slither

slight *adj. I've got a slight problem with my computer.* insignificant, little, minor, small, trivial, unimportant ***major**

slim *adj. She's slim and healthy.* lean, slender, slight, thin, trim, willowy ***fat**

slip *v. I slipped on the wet floor.* fall, glide, skid, slide, tumble

slippery *adj. Be careful when you go into the kitchen; the floor is very slippery.* slithery, smooth ***rough**

slither *v. The snake slithered through the grass.* glide, skate, skim, slink, slip

slope *n. We climbed the steep slope to the castle at the top.* bank, hill, incline, rise

sloppy *adj. Your spelling can be very sloppy.* careless, messy, slapdash (*informal*) ***careful**

slow *adj. We're making very slow progress.* leisurely, sluggish, unhurried ***fast**

sly *adj. Foxes are sly creatures.* artful, crafty, cunning, sneaky, wily

smack *v. She smacked the desk with her palm.* hit, slap, spank, strike, whack (*informal*)

small *adj. They live in a small cottage in the countryside.* compact, cramped, little, tiny ***big**
I'm much smaller than my sister; she's huge! diminutive, petite,

short *tall

There's a small problem with the opera tickets I bought. little, minor, slight, trivial, unimportant *big

smart *adj. This is a really smart class.* alert, bright, clever, intelligent, learned, quick-witted, wise, brainy (*informal*) *stupid

smash *v. I smashed a plate.* break, destroy, shatter, wreck

The car smashed into a lamppost. collide with, crash into, hit, ram into, slam into

smell *n. These rosebushes have a nice smell.* aroma, fragrance, perfume, scent

There's a horrible smell in here. odor, stench, whiff (*informal*)

smile *v. The girl smiled at me.* beam, grin, simper, smirk, sneer *frown

smooth *adj. The surface is smooth.* even, flat, level *rough

The horse had a smooth coat. glossy, shiny, silky, sleek *dull

snack *n. We stopped for a snack.* light meal, refreshments, bite to eat (*informal*)

snatch *v. The thief snatched my bag.* grab, grab ahold of, seize, steal

sneak¹ *n. (informal) You little sneak!* informer (*formal*), snitch (*informal*), tattletale (*informal*), whistleblower (*informal*)

sneak² *v. I sneaked in while no one was looking.* creep, slink, slip, steal

sneaky *adj. That was a very sneaky way of getting people to donate money.* crafty, devious, scheming, sly, underhand, unfair

snobbish *adj. The sitcom is about a snobbish housewife who thinks she's better than her neighbors.* condescending, haughty, patronizing, supercilious, hoity-toity (*informal*), stuck-up (*informal*)

snoop *v. There's been a reporter snooping around outside the restaurant all night.* eavesdrop, meddle, prowl, pry, sneak

so *conj. The weather was nice, so we decided to have a picnic.* accordingly, for that reason, hence, therefore, thus

sob *v. The little girl was sobbing.* bawl, cry, shed tears, weep, blubber (*informal*)

soft *adj. The ground is soft.* soggy, spongy, swampy, squishy (*informal*) *hard

This sweater feels really soft against my skin. fluffy, gentle, silky, smooth, velvety *rough

A soft breeze was blowing. delicate, gentle, light, mild, moderate *strong

He spoke in a soft voice. gentle, hushed, low, quiet, soothing *loud

solid *adj. This cube is a solid object.* dense, firm, hard, rigid, strong, sturdy ***hollow**

solution *n. The solution to the puzzle is at the back of the book.* answer, explanation, key ***question**

solve *v. The detective solved the mystery.* crack, explain, find the answer to, resolve, unravel, figure out (*informal*)

some *adj. There are some people waiting to see the principal.* a few, a group of, a number of, several

sometimes *adv. We sometimes go to see Grandpa on Sundays.* at times, every now and then, from time to time, occasionally ***never**

song *n. What songs will you be singing at the concert?* air, ditty, melody, number, tune

soon *adv. See you soon!* before long, in a little while, presently, shortly

sore *adj. My throat's really sore.* aching, inflamed, painful, raw, tender

sorry *adj. He said he was sorry for breaking the window.* apologetic, regretful, remorseful, repentant
I'm very sorry you're leaving. dejected, distressed, sad, unhappy, upset ***glad**
They felt sorry for the old lady. compassionate, concerned, (full of) pity, sympathetic

sort[1] *n. What sort of flowers do you want?* kind, species, type, variety

sort[2] *v. Could you please sort these papers?* arrange, categorize, classify, organize, put in order

sort out *v. Would you please sort out your things?* clean up, deal with, organize, put in order

sound *n. What's that sound?* bang, din, noise

sour *adj. Lemons are very sour.* acidic, bitter, sharp, tart ***sweet**

space *n. There isn't enough space in here.* area, capacity, expanse, extent, room
There was a space in the fence where the gate had been. gap, opening
There's one space left on the bus for today's field trip. opening, place, spot

spare *adj. Do you have a spare pillow?* additional, another, extra, reserve, surplus
I like reading in my spare time. free, leisure, own

speak *v. I couldn't understand because he was speaking Turkish.* communicate, converse in, talk, utter

special *adj. It's a very special event.* important, momentous, noteworthy, significant, unique ***ordinary**
We have our own special

common room. distinct, individual, particular, specific

speck *n. There's a speck of dust in my eye.* bit, particle, piece

speech *n. The mayor gave a very long speech.* address, lecture, oration, talk

speed *n. We were traveling at a speed of sixty miles per hour.* pace, rate, tempo, velocity

spell *n. The witch had a book of spells.* charm, magic, sorcery, witchcraft
Recently, there's been a spell of good, sunny weather. period, run, stint, stretch, time

spend *v. Nirmala spent $40 at the supermarket.* expend, pay, fork out (*informal*) *****earn
I spent an hour on my homework. devote (to), put in, take, use up

spill *v. Don't spill your juice.* drop, knock over, tip over, upset
Water spilled onto the floor. overflow, pour, run, splash, splatter, stream

spin *v. A top is a toy that spins.* pirouette, revolve, rotate, turn, twist, whirl

spite *n. He did it only out of spite.* hostility, malice,

Spices

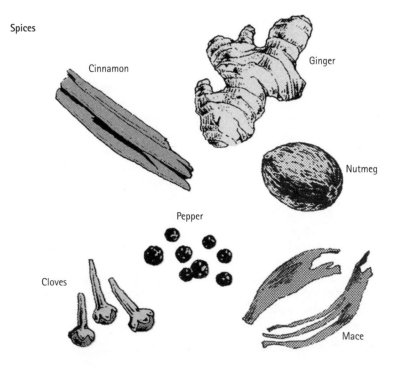

Cinnamon

Ginger

Nutmeg

Pepper

Cloves

Mace

nastiness, rancor, resentment

spiteful *adj. Don't make spiteful remarks about others.* cutting, malicious, mean, nasty, snide, vindictive ***kind**

splash *v. The truck splashed us as it went past.* shower, splatter, spray, sprinkle, wet

split *v. The tree trunk has split.* break, crack, divide, snap, splinter
They split the prize money between them. distribute, divide, share ***combine**

split up *v. Chelsea's parents have split up.* break up, divorce, part, separate ***unite**

spoil *v. The rain spoiled the barbecue.* mar, mess up, ruin, wreck ***improve**
Betty spoils her four grandchildren. indulge, overindulge, pamper ***neglect**

spot[1] *n. Our cat has long brown fur with black spots.* dot, fleck, mark, patch, speck, speckle, stain
This is a good spot for a picnic. location, place, position, site, venue

spot[2] *v. Have you spotted any famous people while you've been waiting here?* catch sight of, glimpse, notice, recognize, see

spray *v. Dad sprayed the roses with weed killer.* shower, sprinkle, squirt

spread *v. Kim spread whipped cream on the top of the cake before she ate it.* apply, put, slather, smear
Mom spread the map out on the table. lay out, open out, unfold, unfurl, unroll ***fold**

spy *n. The FBI believed that there was a spy in the White House.* mole, secret agent

spy on *v. Satellites orbiting Earth are able to spy on all of us.* keep under surveillance, observe, shadow, track the movements of, watch, snoop *(informal)*

squabble *v. My neighbor and I are always squabbling.* argue, bicker, fight, quarrel ***agree**

squash *v. Please squash plastic bottles before putting them in the recycle bin.* compress, crush, flatten, press, squeeze
Ow! You're squashing me! press, push, shove

squeal *v. Robbie squealed at the sight of a mouse running across the kitchen floor.* cry out, scream, screech, shriek, squeak

squeeze *v. Kelly squeezed my arm hard.* clasp, clutch, grasp, pinch, press
We all squeezed onto the sofa. cram, crowd, crush, pack, squash

squirt *v. Water squirted out of the hose.* gush, shoot, splash, spray, spurt

stab *v. The mugger stabbed him with a knife.* jab, knife, pierce, puncture, wound

stable *adj. Make sure the shelf is stable.* firm, secure, solid, steady, strong *****wobbly**
House prices have remained stable for a year. constant, lasting, level, steady, uniform *****varied**

stack *n. A stack of books was at the foot of the bed.* heap, mound, pile

staff *n. The parking lot is for staff only.* crew, employees, personnel, work force

stage *n. This is only the first stage of the inquiry.* part, phase, section, step

stagger *v. The drunk man staggered along the street.* lurch, reel, teeter, totter

stain *n. There's a big brown stain on my tie.* blot, mark, smudge, spot

stamp *v. Clap your hands and stamp your feet in time to the music.* step, stomp, tramp

stand[1] *n. Let's take a stand at the meeting.* side, viewpoint

stand[2] *v. I just can't stand the taste of olives.* bear, endure, put up with, tolerate, stomach (*informal*)

standard[1] *n. The standard of your work has improved.* grade, level, quality

standard[2] *adj. An off-peak ticket costs half the price of a standard ticket.* general, normal, ordinary, typical, usual

stand up *v. We all stood up when the principal came in.* get to one's feet, rise *****sit**
She stood up for her beliefs at the rally. defend, uphold

stare *v. What are you staring at?* gape, gaze, glare, look, peer, gawk (*informal*)

start[1] *n. We had a test at the start of the class.* beginning, commencement, opening, outset *****end**

start[2] *v. Can we start now?* begin, get going, commence (*formal*), kick off (*informal*) *****finish**
I'd like to start my own business. create, establish, found, launch, set up

startle *v. I didn't mean to startle you.* alarm, frighten, scare, surprise

state[1] *n. Iraq is now in a very sorry state.* circumstance, condition, situation

state[2] *v. She had to state her name for the record.* announce, declare, pronounce, say

stay *v. Stay here until I get back.* hold on, pause, remain, wait, hang around (*informal*) *****leave**
The weather stayed warm and sunny all week. continue to be, keep, remain

steal *v. Someone's stolen my bag.* rob, thieve, swipe (*informal*)

steep *adj. We climbed to the top of the steep slope.* precipitous, sheer *****gentle**

step *v. I accidentally stepped on my dog's tail.* stamp, trample, walk

stick¹ *n. We gathered some sticks from the forest to build a fire.* branch, twig

stick² *v. Rebecca stuck the label on the package and then mailed it.* attach, fix, glue, paste
The glitter sticks to your hand. adhere, cling
I closed my eyes and stuck a pin into the map. insert, push, thrust

stick out *v. Evan's front teeth stick out.* jut out, project, protrude

stick up for *v. My brother always sticks up for me.* defend, stand up for, support ***criticize**

sticky *adj. Maple syrup is so sticky!* gloppy, gluey, gummy, syrupy, tacky

stiff *adj. I stuck the picture onto stiff cardboard.* firm, hard, inflexible, rigid, thick ***flexible**
My muscles are stiff. aching, painful, sore, tense

still *adv. Painters' models have to sit still for hours.* calmly, motionlessly

stingy *adj. Ebenezer Scrooge was very stingy.* cheap, miserly, thrifty, penny-pinching (*informal*)

stink *v. This place stinks. What have you been cooking?* smell, reek (*informal*)

stop *v. I wish I could stop smoking.* cease, discontinue, forgo, give up, renounce, quit (*informal*) ***start**
We'll go out when the rain stops. cease, come to an end, conclude, end, finish ***start**
The car stopped quickly at the traffic lights. come to a halt, come to a standstill ***depart**
You can't stop me from going out if I want to. hinder, prevent, restrain, restrict ***allow**

store¹ *n. There are lots of stores downtown.* boutique, emporium, market, retail outlet, shop

store² *v. I store my entire collection of books in the basement.* keep, put, stockpile, stow

storm *n. There have been terrible storms in the Caribbean.* cyclone, gale, hurricane, tornado

story *n. The teacher read the class a story about a gang of pirates.* account, legend, narrative, tale, yarn

straight¹ *adj. The picture isn't straight.* even, level, perpendicular ***crooked**

straight² *adv. Please go straight home without wasting time.* directly, immediately, right, right away

strange *adj. A very strange thing happened today.* curious,

extraordinary, funny, odd,
peculiar, unusual, weird
*ordinary

stream *n. We paddled in the
mountain stream.* brook, river
*A stream of water came out of
the faucet.* gush, jet, spray,
spurt, surge

street *n. Patrick lives on the street
that runs along the side of the
theater.* avenue, boulevard, lane,
road

strength *n. I don't have the
strength to walk up the hill.*
energy, fitness, might, power,
stamina, vigor

stress *n. I feel as if there's too
much stress in my life.* pressure,
strain, tension

stressful *adj. Libby has a very
stressful job at the moment.*
demanding, difficult, taxing,
tiring *easy

stretch *v. He stretched out his
hand.* extend, hold out, offer,
reach out
She stretched the elastic.
elongate, extend, lengthen, pull
(out)

strict *adj. Our teacher is very
strict.* firm, harsh, rigid, severe,
stern

stripe *n. My sweater is blue with
red stripes.* band, bar, line,
streak, strip

stroke *v. Alistair stroked the
kitten.* caress, pat, pet, rub,
touch

strong *adj. Weightlifters are very
strong.* burly, hardy, muscular,
powerful, robust, sturdy,
well built, beefy (*informal*)
*weak
*Wear strong shoes for climbing
mountains.* durable, long
lasting, sturdy, tough
Garlic has a strong taste.
pungent, spicy, tangy

struggle *v. Sammy and Bob
struggled to lift the heavy rock.*
battle, endeavor, labor, strain,
try hard

stubborn *adj. Our dog is so
stubborn and never does what
we want.* disobedient,
headstrong, obstinate, strong
willed, uncooperative, willful

stuck-up *adj. (informal) The
actress has a reputation in
the industry for being stuck-up.*
arrogant, conceited, snobbish,
vain, too big for one's
britches (*informal*)

study *v. The teacher told me that
I should spend more time
studying.* learn, work
Study the picture very carefully.
analyze, evaluate, examine,
investigate

stuff[1] *n. Put your stuff away and
go to bed.* belongings,
equipment, property, things

stuff[2] *v. I quickly stuffed my
books into my school bag and
ran for the bus.* cram, jam,
press, push, ram, shove, thrust

stupid *adj. Please stop this stupid behavior.* foolish, idiotic, ignorant, irresponsible, senseless, unintelligent, dumb (*informal*) ***sensible**

subject *n. The subject of today's lesson is the Russian Revolution.* content, matter, theme, topic

succeed *v. If you work hard in life, then you should succeed.* do well, flourish, prosper, thrive, triumph ***fail**

success *n. The event was a big success.* triumph, hit (*informal*) ***failure**

successful *adj. He's one of the most successful living writers in the entire world.* famous, fortunate, prosperous, thriving

sudden *adj. There was a sudden gust of wind, and then it started to rain.* abrupt, unexpected

suddenly *adv. He suddenly got up from his chair and went out of the room.* abruptly, unexpectedly, without notice, without warning, out of the blue (*informal*) ***gradually**

suffer *v. I really don't like to see anyone suffer.* be distressed, be upset, experience hardship, feel pain, hurt

suggest *v. Rosie suggested going to get a pizza.* advise, propose, recommend
The story suggests that the maid committed the murder. hint, imply, insinuate

suit *v. Do these glasses suit me?* flatter, look good on
Would Monday suit you to hold a meeting? be convenient for, please, satisfy

suitable *adj. That certainly isn't a suitable present for a toddler.* appropriate, apt, fitting, perfect ***unsuitable**
Would next Tuesday be suitable for you to come in and see us? acceptable, convenient, possible, satisfactory

sulk *v. Molly sat sulking in her room.* be in a bad mood, brood, mope, pout

sulky *adj. How can I deal with a sulky teenager?* grumpy, moody, sullen

sunny *adj. It was a lovely sunny day.* bright, clear, fine, nice, warm ***dull**

supply[1] *n. I always keep a secret supply of candy in my drawer.* cache, collection, hoard, reserve, stock

supply[2] *v. The hostel supplies sheets and towels for its guests.* furnish with, give, make available, provide

support *v. Wooden beams support the roof.* bear, hold up, prop up, strengthen
Freddie was the only one of my family and friends who supported me. back, defend, favor, help, stick up for (*informal*) ***criticize**

suppose v. *I suppose you've done your homework already.*
assume, expect, imagine, presume

sure adj. *Are you absolutely sure that the appointment is at nine o'clock in the morning?* certain, confident, convinced, positive
Our team is sure to win. bound, certain, guaranteed, very likely
***unlikely**

surprise[1] n. *The announcement came as a surprise.* shock, bombshell (*informal*)
Saira had a look of absolute surprise on her face.
amazement, astonishment, disbelief, incredulity

surprise[2] v. *The news surprised me.* amaze, astonish, astound, stun, take aback

surrender v. *The soldiers holding the fort will never surrender.*
accept defeat, concede, give up, relinquish, submit, yield

surround v. *The hotel building is surrounded by some of the most beautiful grounds I have ever seen.* encircle, enclose, ring

suspect v. *I suspect he hasn't told his parents yet.* have a feeling, have a hunch, imagine, suppose
***know**

suspicious adj. *She was very suspicious when she saw the lipstick on her husband's collar.*
distrustful, doubtful, dubious, skeptical

swap v. *Should we swap places?*
exchange, switch, trade

sweet adj. *This orange juice is very sweet.* luscious, sugary, syrupy ***sour**
What a sweet little hamster!
adorable, cute, lovable

swing v. *I can see a rope swinging from that tree over there.* dangle, hang, rock, sway

switch[1] n. *Press this switch.*
button, control, key, knob, lever

switch[2] v. *The relatives kept switching cars.* change, exchange, substitute, swap, trade ***keep**

symbol n. *An apple is the symbol of New York City.* emblem, image, sign, token

sympathy n. *I feel great sympathy for the parents of the missing girl.* compassion, concern, pity, understanding

system n. *We've got a brand-new system for checking homework; it should make the job quicker.*
arrangement, method, procedure, routine, technique

Tt

take v. *He took my arm.* clutch, grab, grasp, take hold of
Take this note to the office.
bring, carry, convey

Mom took me to the station. accompany, convey, drive, escort, lead, transport
Take your feet off the chair. move, remove, withdraw
Someone's taken my purse. remove, steal
I take it you're here for an interview. assume, expect, imagine, presume, suppose

take place *v.* *When did the accident take place?* happen, occur, transpire, come to pass (*literary*)

talent *n.* *Lisa has a talent for languages.* ability, aptitude, flair, genius, gift, knack

talented *adj.* *Keith's a talented singer.* able, accomplished, competent, excellent, gifted, skillful

talk¹ *n.* *The school nurse gave a talk on healthy eating.* address, discourse, lecture, speech, spiel (*informal*)

talk² *v.* *My mom and her friends were talking.* chat, communicate, converse, gossip, speak
Don't talk such nonsense! express, say, speak, utter, voice
We've been talking about the new Superman movie. comment on, discuss, refer to, speak about

tall *adj.* *A tall building blocked the sun.* big, high, lofty, towering ***low**

tame *adj.* *The circus animals are all tame.* docile, domesticated, gentle, mild ***wild**

tangled *adj.* *The wool has become tangled.* jumbled, intertwined, knotted, twisted

tap *v.* *He tapped on the window.* knock, pat, rap

target *n.* *We need to set a target of 75 percent.* aim, goal, ideal,

Tame

Although we found it in the woods, the kitten was docile.

137

figure, objective

task *n. I've got one more task to do.* assignment, chore, duty, errand, exercise, job, mission, undertaking

taste¹ *n. I don't like the taste of beets.* flavor, savor, tang
I've made some onion soup; would you like a taste? bit, drop, mouthful, nibble, sample, sip, spoonful

taste² *v. Could you please taste this and tell me if you think it needs more salt?* check, sample, savor, sip, test, try

tasty *adj. The meal was very tasty.* appetizing, delicious, full of flavor, scrumptious (*informal*), yummy (*informal*) ***disgusting**

teach *v. Alison teaches children in first grade.* coach, educate, instruct, train, tutor

teacher *n. I want to be a teacher when I grow up.* coach, educator, instructor, lecturer, professor, trainer, tutor

team *n. Members of the team should arrive as early as possible.* crew, group, squad

tear *v. I tried very hard not to tear my tights as I took them off.* rip, snag, split, rend (*literary*)

tease *v. Some children teased Monica because of her accent.* laugh at, make fun of, mock, poke fun at, ridicule, taunt, torment

tell *v. You must tell your parents if you're going to be home late.* inform, notify, warn
Please tell me about your weekend. describe, inform, recount, relate, talk
Mrs. Patel told me to rewrite my story. ask, command, instruct, order
My mom told me how to make pancakes. describe, explain, instruct, show, teach
It's a secret, so it's very important that you don't tell your parents about this. divulge, reveal, blab (*informal*), spill the beans (*informal*)

temper *n. Dad has a bad temper.* disposition, temperament

temporary *adj. It's only a temporary classroom.* interim, provisional, short-term ***permanent**

tempt *v. Can I tempt you to have a chocolate?* cajole, convince, entice, persuade

tempting *adj. Those cakes look tempting.* appealing, appetizing, attractive, delicious, inviting, irresistible, mouthwatering

tend *v. I tend to watch television at night.* be apt, be inclined, be likely, prefer
The residents of the nursing home tend the garden every day as part of their exercise. attend to, cultivate, look after, maintain, take care of ***neglect**

tense *adj. My muscles are tense.* sore, stiff, strained, taut, tight
I was feeling very tense as I sat outside the principal's office. anxious, edgy, nervous, on edge, uneasy, worried *calm
It's a tense thriller set in China. dramatic, exciting, suspenseful, thrilling *boring

terrible *adj. We saw a terrible accident on the highway.* appalling, awful, dreadful, horrible, serious, shocking

terrific *adj. Someone was making a terrific bang outside.* huge, loud, tremendous
That was a terrific film. amazing, excellent, fantastic, great, outstanding, superb, tremendous *terrible

test[1] *n. We have a math test today.* assessment, exam, examination

test[2] *v. Scientists have to test new medicines very carefully, in case they could be dangerous.* analyze, check, examine, experiment with, investigate, try out

thaw *v. The ice is beginning to thaw.* dissolve, liquefy, melt, soften *set

theft *n. He's in prison for theft.* burglary, embezzlement, robbery

theme *n. The theme of the painting is freedom.* central idea, motif, subject, subject matter, topic

theory *n. Do you believe my theory about the accident?* conjecture, hypothesis, speculation

therefore *adv. I ate too much cake; therefore I got sick.* accordingly, consequently, hence

thick *adj. He cut a thick slice of bread.* big, chunky, hefty, large *thin
The walls are very thick. dense, solid, wide *thin

thief *n. The police caught the thief red-handed at the scene of the crime.* burglar, criminal, mugger, pickpocket, robber, shoplifter, crook (*informal*)

thin *adj. Sabrina is looking very thin at the moment.* lean, skinny, slender, slight, slim *fat
Draw a thin black line. fine, narrow *wide
Lorna is wearing a thin jacket. delicate, flimsy, light, lightweight *thick

thing *n. There are lots of interesting things in the museum.* article, item, object

things *n. pl. You can keep your things in the locker.* belongings, equipment, gear, possessions, property, personal effects (*formal*)

think *v. I thought it was a very touching movie.* believe,

consider, have the impression,
judge
Leave me alone; I'm thinking.
concentrate, contemplate,
daydream, meditate, muse,
ponder, reflect

thirsty *adj. I'm thirsty; is there
anything to drink?* dehydrated,
dry, parched (*informal*)

though[1] *conj. They've gone to the
store, though they don't have any
money.* although, despite the
fact that, even though

though[2] *adv. Andrew is looking
for a Saturday job; he's only 15,
though, which could be a
problem.* anyhow, having said
that, however, nevertheless

thought *n. Chris sat at the desk
in his office, deep in thought.*
concentration, contemplation,
reflection, study
*Some new thoughts on the
subject have just occurred to me.*
concept, idea, notion, brain
wave (*informal*)

thoughtful *adj. Sally is a very
thoughtful girl; she always
considers others.* caring,
considerate, helpful, kind,
sympathetic ***thoughtless**
*Why are you looking so
thoughtful? What is on your
mind must be really important.*
contemplative, deep in thought,
engrossed, pensive, reflective,
studious

thoughtless *adj. Honestly, José,*

*you can be really thoughtless
at times.* careless, heedless,
inconsiderate, indiscreet,
insensitive, tactless
***thoughtful**

threaten *v. The teenagers
threatened the storekeeper.*
bully, frighten, intimidate,
menace

thrill *n. The thrill of winning is
the main reason I compete.*
enjoyment, excitement, fun,
buzz (*informal*), kick (*informal*)

thrilling *adj. The movie told a
thrilling story.* action packed,
exciting, gripping, stimulating
***boring**

throw *v. I threw a ball, and the
dog ran after it.* cast, fling, hurl,
pitch, chuck (*informal*) ***catch**

throw away *v. I threw away all of
my old clothes because I was
running out of closet space.*
clear out, discard, dispose of,
get rid of, chuck out (*informal*)
***preserve**

tidy *adj. You should always keep
your desk tidy.* in good order,
neat, orderly, shipshape, well
kept ***messy**

tie *v. Tie these two ribbons
together.* attach, fasten, fix,
join, knot, secure ***undo**

tight[1] *adj. Keep a tight hold on
the banister.* careful, firm,
secure
*My pants are much too
tight.* close fitting, small,

Titles

Admiral
Ambassador
Archbishop
Baron
Baroness
Brigadier
Cardinal
Chancellor
Colonel
Constable
Count
Countess
Czar
Czarina
Dame
Deacon
Dean
Don
Doña
Duchess
Duke
Earl
Emir
Emperor
General
Governor
Infanta
Kaiser
Khan
King
Knight
Lady
Lama
Lieutenant
Lord
Madame
Maharajah
Maharani
Major
Mandarin
Marchioness
Margrave
Marshal
Master
Mayor
Mikado
Miss
Mogul
Monsieur
Monsignor
Pasha
Pope
Priest
Prince
Princess
Queen
Rabbi
Regent
Senator
Señor
Señora
Señorita
Sergeant
Shah
Sheik
Sheriff
Shogun
Signor
Signora
Signorina
Sir
Sultan
Sultana
Vicar
Viceroy
Viscount
Viscountess

141

tight fitting *loose

tight[2] *adv. Make sure the string is pulled tight.* stretched, taut, tense

tilt *v. Don't tilt your chairs back.* incline, lean, slant, slope, tip

time *n. The 1500s were a time of discovery.* age, epoch, era, period
After a time, the teacher stood up. interval, period, spell, stint
What's the best time of day to call you? moment, occasion, point

tiny *adj. Ladybugs are tiny creatures.* diminutive, microscopic, minuscule, minute, small *huge

tip *n. Only the very tip of an iceberg is ever visible above the water.* apex, peak, point, summit, top *base

tired *adj. I'm tired; I need to rest.* drained, exhausted, sleepy, weary, worn out *lively
I'm tired of listening to your excuses. bored with, fed up with

together *adv. The whole class sang together.* as one, collectively, in unison, jointly, simultaneously *alone

too *adv. This is too difficult.* excessively, extremely, overly, unduly
Can I come too? also, as well, besides, in addition

tool *n. The plumber carried all of his tools in a metal box.* device, gadget, implement, instrument, utensil

top[1] *n. We climbed to the top of the mountain.* apex, crest, peak, pinnacle, summit *base
I can't get the top off this jar. cap, cover, lid
My top doesn't match my pants. blouse, shirt, sweater, sweatshirt, T-shirt

top[2] *adj. She is one of the country's top athletes.* best, finest, foremost, greatest, leading *worst

topic *n. What topic have you chosen for your school project?* issue, subject, subject matter, theme

torment *v. My little brother is always tormenting our pet rabbits.* annoy, irritate, pester, tease

total *adj. The total number of visitors per year was on the rise.* combined, complete, entire
We had to sit in total silence. absolute, complete, perfect, utter

touch *v. I touched the velvet material; it felt very soft.* feel, finger, fondle, handle, pat, stroke
Please don't touch any of the paintings or sculptures that I have put on display. handle, lay a finger on, meddle with, pick up, fiddle with (*informal*)

tough *adj. This plastic is very tough.* durable, hard, long lasting, robust, rugged, strong, sturdy ***weak***
The obstacle course was tough. arduous, demanding, difficult, grueling ***easy***
In the movie he plays a tough guy. rough, rowdy, ruthless, violent ***gentle***

town *n. My town has a population of 15,000 people.* city, metropolis, suburb, village

trace *v. Police are trying to trace the missing girl.* discover, find, track down ***lose***

track[1] *n. Donna cycled along the track.* path, pathway, trail

track[2] *v. The hunters tracked the animal for more than ten miles.* chase, follow, pursue, search out, stalk, trace

trade *v. I'll trade my chocolate bar for your bag of chips.* barter, exchange, swap, switch

tragedy *n. Dozens of people were injured in the tragedy.* accident, calamity, catastrophe, disaster

train *v. Jenny trains people at work how to use the computer system.* coach, educate,

Toys

Wheeled toy, ancient Egypt

Top and whip, 1700s

Doll, 1900s

Electronic game, 2000s

instruct, teach, tutor
The baseball team trains three times a week. exercise, practice, work out

traitor *n. Those found guilty of being traitors were shot during the war.* double agent, spy, turncoat (*informal*)

trap¹ *n. The fox tried to run away, but it got caught in a trap.* ambush, net, pitfall, snare

trap² *v. The poachers trapped a hare in their snares.* bag, capture, catch, corner, ensnare, snare ***release**

travel *v. My cousin is traveling around the world by land and sea; he won't be taking any planes.* explore, journey, tour, trek, voyage

treasure¹ *n. The pirates buried the treasure.* riches, valuables

treasure² *v. I really treasure my freedom.* appreciate, cherish, esteem, prize, value

treat *v. The owners of the company had always treated the staff very badly.* deal with, handle, manage
My grandma treated me to an expensive meal at a fancy restaurant. entertain, invite, take someone out for

tremble *v. I woke up trembling with fear.* quake, quiver, shake, shiver, shudder

tremendous *adj. I heard a tremendous bang.* almighty, deafening, enormous, huge, immense, loud, resounding ***tiny**
The team has had a tremendous year. excellent, outstanding, superb, wonderful ***poor**

trick¹ *n. She played a mean trick on me.* hoax, practical joke, prank

trick² *v. He tricked people into thinking that he was a millionaire.* cheat, deceive, fool, hoodwink, mislead

trickle *v. Water trickled from a crack in the pipe.* dribble, drip, leak, ooze, seep

tricky *adj. I found myself in a tricky situation.* awkward, delicate, difficult, embarrassing

trim *v. Mom trimmed Dad's hair.* clip, crop, cut, shorten

trip¹ *n. We went on a field trip to the zoo.* excursion, expedition, jaunt, journey, outing, tour

trip² *v. I tripped on a loose stone.* fall, lose one's balance, slip, stumble

trouble¹ *n. I had trouble finding a hotel in which to stay.* difficulty, inconvenience, problem, hassle (*informal*)
There was trouble outside the school late last night. disorder, disturbance, fighting, problems, unrest
I don't want to bore you with all of my troubles. misfortune,

problem, worry

trouble² v. *I'm terribly sorry to trouble you about something so trivial.* annoy, bother, disturb, inconvenience

true adj. *Is it true that the supermarket is closing down?* accurate, correct, right, the case *****false
The movie is based on a true story. actual, authentic, factual, genuine, real *****imaginary

trust v. *I'm really not sure whether I can trust the car salesman.* believe in, depend on, have confidence in, rely on *****doubt

truth n. *Do you think there's any truth to the rumor?* accuracy, fact, honesty, reality *****lie

try v. *I'm trying to find a job.* attempt, endeavor, make an effort, strive
You'll have a chance to try different sports to see if you like them. sample, test

turn v. *The Sun stays still and Earth turns.* go around, pivot, revolve, rotate, spin, whirl

turn down v. *I turned down the invitation.* decline, refuse, say no to *****accept

turn into v. *In the story, a man turns into a giant insect.* become, be transformed into, change into, develop into, metamorphose into (*formal*)

twist v. *The road twisted and*

turned for many miles. bend, curve, meander, zigzag
The taxi driver twisted around to talk to us. pivot, swivel, turn, twirl
Twist one strand of hair over another to make a braid. coil, intertwine, weave, wind

type n. *What type of tree is this?* category, genus, kind, sort, species

typical adj. *A typical day for me begins at seven o'clock.* average, normal, ordinary, standard, usual *****unusual

Uu

ugly adj. *The new skyscraper is a very ugly building.* hideous, unattractive, unpleasant, unsightly *****beautiful

unable adj. *We can offer advice but are unable to book tickets for you.* helpless, incapable, not authorized, not permitted, powerless *****able

unaware adj. *I was unaware that there was a café in this building.* ignorant, oblivious *****aware

unbearable adj. *I find this hot weather unbearable.* impossible, intolerable, unacceptable *****pleasant

unbelievable adj. *The transfer fee is unbelievable.* amazing, beyond belief, incredible, mind-boggling (*informal*)

uncertain *adj. She's uncertain whether to study German or Spanish in college.* doubtful, unclear, undecided, unsure ***certain**

The immediate future of the car factory is uncertain. in doubt, in limbo, unknown, up in the air (*informal*) ***certain**

uncomfortable *adj. I often feel uncomfortable when I meet someone new.* awkward, embarrassed, ill at ease, self-conscious, uneasy, worried ***comfortable**

unconscious *adj. The patient was unconscious.* comatose, in a coma, knocked out, out cold (*informal*) ***lively**

Nail biting is an unconscious habit. automatic, instinctive, involuntary, unintentional, unplanned

uncover *v. Police have uncovered a plot to rob a bank.* discover, expose, find, reveal, stumble upon, unearth

under *prep. Everything at this store costs under $1.* below, less than, lower than

Have you looked under your bed? below, beneath, underneath

understand *v. I couldn't understand everything he said.* comprehend, follow, grasp, keep up with, take in

I understand how difficult it is for you. appreciate, know, realize, recognize, sympathize

undo *v. I can't undo this knot.* disentangle, open, release, separate, unfasten, untie ***fasten**

uneven *adj. The ground is a little uneven.* bumpy, lopsided, lumpy, rough ***flat**

It was an uneven contest; the pros were playing the amateurs. lopsided, one-sided, unbalanced, unfair ***fair**

unexpected *adj. She paid us an unexpected visit.* chance, impulsive, sudden, unforeseen, unplanned

unfair *adj. Some people think that the prison system is unfair.* discriminatory, one-sided, prejudiced, unjust, wrong ***fair**

unfaithful *adj. Mary discovered that her husband had been unfaithful.* adulterous, disloyal, faithless, two-faced, two-timing (*informal*) ***faithful**

unfamiliar *adj. I was surrounded by a crowd of unfamiliar faces.* alien, foreign, new, strange, unknown ***familiar**

unfasten *v. Please do not unfasten your seat belts until the plane has come to a complete stop.* open, release, unbuckle, undo, untie ***fasten**

unfit *adj. The restaurant was fined for supplying food that was*

unfit for human consumption.
inappropriate to, unsuitable for,
unsuited to *suitable

unfortunate *adj. We were
very unfortunate not to win.*
jinxed, unlucky *fortunate

unfriendly *adj. The students at my
new school are more unfriendly
than at my old school.* aloof,
antagonistic, cold, hostile,
standoffish, surly, unwelcoming
*friendly

ungrateful *adj. A lot of people think
she's a rude and ungrateful girl.*
selfish, thankless, unappreciative,
ungracious *grateful

unhappiness *n. People often try
to hide their unhappiness from
those around them.* depression,
despair, misery, sadness
*happiness

unhappy *adj. My granddad's
childhood was very unhappy.*
dismal, miserable, sad,
wretched *happy

unhealthy *adj. Smoking is an
unhealthy habit.* damaging,
detrimental, harmful, injurious
*healthy
He looks pale and unhealthy.
ill, in poor health, sick, unwell
*healthy

uniform *adj. In some countries in
Europe, tax is applied at a
uniform rate of 20 percent.*
consistent, fixed, invariable,
unchanging *varied

union *n. The United States is a*

union of 50 states. alliance,
association, federation

unite *v. In 1707 the countries of
Scotland and England united to
form Great Britain.*
amalgamate, combine, join,
merge *separate

universal *adj. One of the United
Nations' goals is to achieve
universal education.* across-the-
board, all-embracing, general,
global, worldwide

unkind *adj. I don't like it when
people are unkind to animals.*
callous, cruel, heartless,
inconsiderate, mean, spiteful,
vicious *kind

unknown *adj. The Tomb of the
Unknown Soldier can be seen in
Philadelphia.* anonymous,
nameless, unidentified,
unnamed *famous

unlikely *adj. In the unlikely event
that a fire breaks out, please
leave the building immediately.*
doubtful, far-fetched,
implausible, improbable,
remote, unimaginable *likely

unlucky *adj. I'm so unlucky;
I've never won a thing in my life.*
jinxed, luckless, unfortunate
*lucky

unnatural *adj. The blond color
that Jodie has put in her hair
looks very unnatural.* artificial,
bizarre, fake, odd, synthetic,
unreal, weird *natural

unpleasant *adj. He's an*

unpleasant person. disagreeable, mean, mean-spirited, nasty, objectionable, obnoxious ***pleasant**

unpopular *adj. Poor William! He's the most unpopular boy in his class.* detested, disliked, friendless, shunned ***popular**

unreal *adj. Fairy tales are generally set in an unreal world.* fanciful, fictitious, imaginary, make-believe, pretend ***real**

unruly *adj. There are no unruly students at this school.* disorderly, disruptive, rowdy, uncontrollable ***obedient**

unselfish *adj. The volunteers at the summer camp showed cooperative and unselfish attitudes.* altruistic, charitable, generous, kind, selfless ***selfish**

unsuitable *adj. Many websites on the Internet are unsuitable for children.* improper, inappropriate, unacceptable ***suitable**

untrue *adj. The rumors were untrue.* false, inaccurate, made up, unfounded

unusual *adj. It's an unusual building.* atypical, curious, odd, strange, unconventional ***ordinary**

unwilling *adj. They were unwilling to help.* averse, disinclined, loath, reluctant ***willing**

uproar *n. When Mom got home from work, she found the house in a state of uproar.* chaos, confusion, disorder, mayhem, turmoil ***peace**
Neighbors complained about the uproar. clamor, din, hubbub, noise, racket (*informal*) ***peace**

upset[1] *v. The sight of the dead mouse upset her.* dismay, distress, disturb, perturb, unsettle ***calm**

upset[2] *adj. She was so upset at the news that she burst into tears.* dismayed, distressed, disturbed, hurt, perturbed, saddened, unsettled ***pleased**

urge[1] *n. I had the sudden urge to spend lots of money.* compulsion, desire, wish

urge[2] *v. Because of his grades, the teachers urged him to apply for college.* advise, beseech, encourage, entreat, plead, prod, spur

urgent *adj. The matter is urgent.* critical, crucial, high-priority, important ***petty**

use[1] *n. (yoos) What's the use of learning Latin? Nobody speaks it today.* advantage, benefit, point, purpose, sense, value

use[2] *v. (yooz) What do you use to clean your shoes?* apply, employ, utilize
Can you use a computer? handle, operate, work

He's very sneaky and uses other people exploit, manipulate, take advantage of

useful *adj. This is a very useful gadget.* convenient, effective, handy, helpful, practical
*useless

useless *adj. Some doctors believe that taking vitamins is useless.* a waste of time, futile, ineffective, pointless *effective
I'm useless at math. (*informal*) bad, hopeless, incompetent
*wonderful

use up *v. We've used up all of the milk that was in the fridge.* consume, deplete, drink, exhaust, expend

usual *adj. Our usual driver is sick today.* customary, everyday, familiar, habitual, normal, regular

usually *adv. We usually have fish and chips on Fridays.* almost always, as a rule, generally, more often than not, normally
*seldom

Vv

vacant *adj. The room is vacant.* empty, free, unoccupied
*occupied

vague *adj. I've got a vague idea of what I'm going to write about when I start my novel.* approximate, general, hazy, imprecise, incomplete, rough
*clear

vain *adj. Snow White's stepmother was a very vain woman.* arrogant, conceited, egotistical, self-absorbed, self-centered, selfish, stuck-up (*informal*) *modest

valid *adj. You may leave the school premises only if you have a valid reason.* authentic, genuine, official, proper, verifiable

valuable *adj. This necklace is very valuable.* costly, expensive, precious, priceless, prized
*worthless
Everyone has made a valuable contribution to the charity. beneficial, constructive, important, useful, worthwhile
*worthless

value[1] *n. We didn't realize the value of the ring.* cost, price, worth

value[2] *v. Experts valued the painting at $10,000.* assess, estimate, price, put a price on
I really value all of your comments and feedback. appreciate, hold in high esteem, prize, treasure, welcome

vanish *v. The shadowy figure vanished.* depart, disappear, evaporate, fade away, go away
*appear

varied *adj. This luxury gift basket*

contains a varied selection of food. assorted, diverse, miscellaneous, mixed ***uniform**

variety *n. The basket contains a variety of food.* array, assortment, mixture, range, selection

There are so many different varieties of pasta, each one suited to different sauces. category, class, genus, kind, sort, species, type

various *adj. Screwdrivers are available in various sizes.* different, differing, diverse, many, varied ***same**

vary *v. Prices vary depending on the size.* alter, change, differ, fluctuate ***match**

verdict *n. What was the jury's verdict?* conclusion, decision, finding, judgment, opinion

verify *v. I cannot verify his alibi.* confirm, corroborate, prove, substantiate

version *n. It's a modern version of a traditional fairy tale.* adaptation, copy, interpretation, rendering, variant

Vehicles

Ambulance	Limousine
Automobile	Motorcycle
Bicycle	Ricksha
Bulldozer	Scooter
Bus	Sedan
Cab	Stagecoach
Car	Tank
Cart	Taxi
Chariot	Tractor
Coach	Train
Fire engine	Tram
Go-cart	Trap
Hearse	Trolley
Jeep	Truck

very *adv. I'm reading a very interesting book at the moment.* absolutely, especially, exceedingly, exceptionally, extremely, really *****fairly**

vibrate *v. The washing machine vibrates noisily.* quiver, shake, shudder, tremble

vicious *adj. It was a vicious attack.* brutal, callous, cold-blooded, ferocious, savage, violent *****gentle**

victim *n. Victims were taken to the hospital.* casualty, injured person, sufferer

victory *n. The team earned an impressive victory that week.* achievement, conquest, success, triumph, win

view *n. There's a lovely view from the window.* aspect, outlook, panorama, scene, sight, vista
In my view, circuses shouldn't use animals. belief, estimation, opinion, point of view, viewpoint

vile *adj. His boss is a vile man.* bad, mean, nasty, unpleasant *****pleasant**

violent *adj. Violent criminals are usually sent to prison for a long time.* aggressive, brutal, destructive, ruthless, vicious *****gentle**
There was a violent storm last night. destructive, forceful, intense, powerful, raging,

strong *****gentle**

visible *adj. The horizon was just visible.* apparent, clear, discernible, in sight, in view, noticeable, perceptible *****invisible**

visit *v. We usually visit my grandparents on weekends.* go to see, pay a visit to, drop in on (*informal*)

visitor *n. We're expecting a visitor this morning.* caller, guest

vital *adj. It's vital that you take a form of identification with you when you go to open a bank account.* crucial, essential, imperative, important, indispensable, necessary *****optional**

voluntary *adj. The activities are all voluntary.* intentional, noncompulsory, optional *****compulsory**
I do voluntary work at the thrift store on Saturdays. unpaid, unrewarded, unsalaried *****professional**

vote *n. We'll hold a vote on the matter.* ballot, election, poll, referendum

vote for *v. I voted for Muna to be the team captain.* choose, elect, opt for, select

voyage *n. An around-the-world voyage would be incredible.* expedition, journey, tour, trek, trip

vulgar *adj. Most people try not to use vulgar language in* *public.* coarse, crude, indecent, indelicate, obscene, rude, tasteless ***elegant**

Ww

wage *n. My dad earns a good wage.* earnings, fee, income, pay, remuneration, salary

wait *v. Please wait here until I get back.* linger, remain, stay, stay put, stick around (*informal*) ***leave**

walk[1] *n. Over the weekend we went for a pleasant walk.* amble, hike, ramble, saunter, stroll

walk[2] *v. The children walked very slowly along the path.* amble, ramble, saunter, stroll, wander, mosey (*informal*)
She is walking quickly to the station. march, stride, leg it (*informal*)
We walked for hours. hike, roam, stroll, wander

wander *v. We wandered around the Museum of Modern Art all afternoon.* amble, drift, roam, saunter, stroll, walk, putter (*informal*)
The toddler wandered off from his parents when no one was looking. disappear, get lost, go astray, go missing

want *v. I want to be a doctor.* crave, desire, dream, hope, long
Do you want a drink? care for, feel like, need, require

war *n. The congregation prayed for an end to war.* bloodshed, combat, conflict, fighting, hostilities, military action, strife ***peace**

warm *adj. The water is warm.* hot, lukewarm, tepid ***cool**
It was a warm June day. balmy, fine, hot, mild, pleasant, sunny, tropical ***cool**
Put on a warm jacket. padded, thick, winter, woolly ***light**
You'll be guaranteed a warm welcome. cordial, enthusiastic, fond, friendly, genial, hospitable ***unfriendly**

warn *v. Police warned drivers to slow down.* admonish, advise, inform, remind, tell

warning *n. There's a health warning on cigarette packages.* advice, caution, information
The teacher gave us a test without warning. forewarning, hint, notice, tip-off (*informal*)

wash *v. The floor is dirty; I'd better wash it.* clean, cleanse, mop, rinse, scrub

waste *v. I've wasted so much money on lottery tickets.* squander, throw away, blow (*informal*) ***save**

watch *v. I watched two squirrels playing in the trees.* eye, gaze at, look at, observe, see,

study, witness

I need to watch my diet. bear in mind, be careful about, keep an eye on, pay attention to ***ignore

wave** v. *Larry waved to me.* gesture, signal

The demonstrators were waving flags. brandish, flourish, shake

way n. *Grilling is a healthy way to cook chicken.* method, procedure, process, technique

Can you please tell me the way to the station? direction, route

weak adj *I still feel a little weak from my illness.* delicate, feeble, frail, puny, shaky ***strong**

She made a weak excuse about having to wash her hair. feeble, flimsy, implausible, unconvincing, lame (*informal*), pathetic (*informal*)

wealth n. *He used all of his great wealth to set up a charity.* fortune, funds, money,

Weather Conditions

Hot weather
drought, heat wave, hot, humid, muggy, sultry, sweltering, torrid, tropical

Overcast weather
cloudy, dark, foggy, hazy, misty, murky, overcast, smoggy

Windy weather
blustery, breeze, drafty, flurry, gale, gusty, hurricane, tornado, turbulent, windy

Cold weather
arctic, bitter, blizzard, brisk, chilly, cold, cold snap, cool, freezing, frost, glacial, hail, icy, subzero

Wet weather
deluge
downpour
drizzle
precipitation
rainy
showers
sleet
slush
snowing
soaking

riches *poverty
She wore diamonds, furs, and
other symbols of wealth.
affluence, luxury, opulence,
prosperity *poverty
wealthy *adj. He comes from*
a very wealthy family.
affluent, prosperous, rich,
well-to-do *poor

wear off *v. The results of the*
medicine soon wore off.
decrease, diminish, dwindle,
fade, lessen

welcome *v. The receptionist*
welcomed the guests. greet,
meet, receive

well[1] *adj. I've been sick, but I'm*
feeling well today. fine, fit,
healthy, robust *sick

well[2] *adv. He speaks German very*
well. competently, excellently,
skillfully *poorly
The company treats its staff
very well. decently, fairly,
generously, kindly, properly
*poorly

well-known *adj. We had a visit*
from a well-known scientist.
celebrated, famous, leading,
notable, prominent *unknown

wet[1] *v. You need to wet the soil*
before planting the seeds.
dampen, moisten, soak, spray,
water

wet[2] *adj. The ground is wet.*
damp, drenched, moist,
saturated, soaked, soggy *dry
They're forecasting wet weather.

drizzly, rainy, showery *fine
whine *v. The dog whined for most*
of the journey. groan, howl,
wail, whimper
Alice is always whining about
something. (*informal*) complain,
grumble, moan *praise

whip *v. The rider whipped the*
horse to make it run faster.
flog, lash, thrash

whisper *v. He whispered*
something in my ear. mumble,
murmur, mutter, speak softly
*shout

whole *adj. The whole class was*
kept after school. complete,
entire, full, total

wicked *adj. Hansel and Gretel*
arrived at the house of the
wicked witch. bad, evil, hateful,
immoral, murderous, sinful,
vile *good
It was a wicked party. (*informal*)
amazing, enjoyable, excellent,
great *pathetic

wide *adj. To the right of the living*
room is a wide hallway. broad,
extensive, large, roomy,
spacious, vast *narrow
The store sells a wide range of
goods. comprehensive,
extensive, full, large *narrow

wiggle *v. The baby was wiggling*
in the bathtub. squirm, twist,
writhe

wild *adj. I saw a television show*
about wild animals. ferocious,
fierce, savage, untamed *tame

It was a very wild party. disorderly, riotous, rowdy, uncontrolled, unrestrained, unruly ***peaceful**

willing *adj. Samantha is always willing to help.* eager, game, glad, prepared, ready ***unwilling**

win *v. I hope you win on Saturday.* be successful, come in first, finish first, succeed, triumph ***lose**

wind *v. The river winds through the valley.* bend, coil, curve, meander, turn, twist, weave, zigzag

windy *adj. It was a windy day.* blustery, breezy

winner *n. The winner was presented with a silver trophy.* champion, hero, victor

wipe *v. Wipe the counter when you're finished.* clean, mop, rub, wash

wisdom *n. Solomon was well known for his wisdom.* intelligence, judgment, knowledge, shrewdness

wise *adj. I don't think that's a very wise decision.* astute, prudent, sensible, shrewd, smart, sound, well advised ***silly**

The old woman was very wise. experienced, full of knowledge, intelligent

wish¹ *n. The genie granted Aladdin three wishes.* ambition, command, desire, request

wish² *v. He wished that he could sing well.* desire, dream, want

wither *v. The flowers withered because nobody watered them.* die, fade, shrivel up, wilt

witness *n. There were several witnesses to the accident.* bystander, eyewitness, observer, onlooker, spectator

witty *adj. He wrote a very witty article.* amusing, clever, comical, entertaining, funny, humorous ***boring**

wobble *v. My chair wobbles.* jiggle, rock, sway, teeter

wobbly *adj. The table is wobbly.* precarious, shaky, unstable, unsteady ***stable**

woman *n. That woman is very pretty.* female, girl, lady, gal (*informal*)

wonder¹ *n. Everyone gazed in wonder at the amazing view.* admiration, amazement, astonishment, awe, surprise

wonder² *v. I asked because I was just wondering.* be curious, consider, muse, ponder, speculate, think

wonderful *adj. We had a wonderful time.* delightful, fabulous, fantastic, great, marvelous, splendid, super, superb ***terrible**

work¹ *n. Chopping wood is very hard work.* drudgery, labor, toil, grind (*informal*)

The teacher gave us some work.
assignment, chore, job, project,
task

work² *v. They worked all night.*
exert, labor, slave (away), toil
*rest

*The washing machine doesn't
work.* function, go, operate, run

world *n. This product is sold all
over the world.* earth, globe,
planet

worried *adj. Sylvia was worried
because her son hadn't called.*
anxious, concerned, distraught,
on edge, upset ***relieved**

worry¹ *n. He's got money worries.*
concern, difficulty, problem,
trouble, headache (*informal*)

worry² *v. His attitude worries me.*
alarm, annoy, bother, cause
anxiety to, concern, distress,
disturb, trouble ***please**

*She worries when she's home
alone.* be anxious, fret, get
flustered, panic ***relax**

worse *adj. My grade was worse
than Rory's.* inferior, lesser, less
good, lower ***better**

worst *adj. It's the worst movie
that I've ever seen.* most awful,
most terrible ***best**

worth *n. Don't underestimate
your own worth to the team.*
benefit, importance, merit,
value, virtue

worthless *adj. Experts said that
the painting was worthless.*
cheap, inexpensive, of little

value, valueless ***valuable**

worthwhile *adj. All of your hard
work has been worthwhile.*
beneficial, fruitful, helpful,
useful, valuable ***useless**

wound¹ *n. The nurse put a
bandage on the wound.* cut,
gash, injury

wound² *v. Several people have
been wounded in a train crash.*
harm, hurt, injure

wrap *v. I wrapped the present in
silver paper.* cover, enclose, pack
(up) ***open**

wreck *v. The tornado wrecked
several buildings.* damage,
demolish, destroy, ruin, smash,
spoil ***build**

write *v. I wrote down my address.*
inscribe, make a note of, note
down, scrawl, scribble, jot
down (*informal*)

*Our homework is to write a
poem.* compose, create, pen,
produce, think up

writer *n. We had a lecture by
a well-known writer.* author,
dramatist, novelist, playwright,
poet

wrong *adj. Stealing is wrong.* illegal,
immoral, sinful, wicked ***right**

*I was wrong about the date;
it's next Tuesday.* inaccurate,
incorrect, inexact, mistaken
*right

*I knew that I'd said the wrong
thing.* inappropriate, incorrect,
unsuitable ***right**

Yy

yell *v. We could hear our neighbors yelling at each other.* roar, scream, screech, shout, shriek

yellow *adj. Timothy is wearing a yellow T-shirt.* amber, gold, golden, lemon

young *adj. A group of young men went on a road trip.* adolescent, immature, junior, teenage, youthful *****old**

Zz

zero *n. I scored zero on the test.* nothing, nada (*informal*), zilch (*informal*), zip (*informal*)

zone *n. Vehicles aren't allowed in the pedestrian zone.* area, district, quarter, sector

zoom *v. The car zoomed through the streets.* dash, flash, hurtle, speed, streak, tear (*informal*), whiz (*informal*) *****dawdle**